Unfettering Confession

Ritualized Performance in Spanish Narrative and Drama

Donald Gene Pace

University Press of America,® Inc.
Lanham · Boulder · New York · Toronto · Plymouth, UK

Copyright © 2009 by
University Press of America,® Inc.
4501 Forbes Boulevard
Suite 200
Lanham, Maryland 20706
UPA Acquisitions Department (301) 459-3366

Estover Road
Plymouth PL6 7PY
United Kingdom

All rights reserved
Printed in the United States of America
British Library Cataloging in Publication Information Available

Library of Congress Control Number: 2008942467
ISBN-13: 978-0-7618-4510-2 (paperback : alk. paper)
eISBN-13: 978-0-7618-4511-9

♾™ The paper used in this publication meets the minimum
requirements of American National Standard for Information
Sciences—Permanence of Paper for Printed Library Materials,
ANSI Z39.48—1984

To Deone

Table of Contents

Preface vii

Acknowledgements ix

Chapter One 1
Liberating a Captive Genre: Past Insights and New Perspectives
    Establishing the Confessional Subject 1
    St. Augustine 2
    Santa Teresa de Jesús 3
    Jean-Jacques Rousseau 3
    The Theorists' Legacy (Root, Tentler) 4
    Beyond Guilt and Religious Confession (Root, Tentler) 4
    A Genre of Crisis: From Humiliation to Hope (Zambrano, S. M. Levin) 6
    The Confessional Hero and the Quest for Self-discovery (Axthelm) 7
    The Author as Confessant (Chacel) 7
    The Appeal to an Audience: Confession and Society (Doody) 8
    A Perlocutionary Ritual: The Search for Reaffirmation and Healing (Foster) 8
    The Pattern of Death and Rebirth (Rosenberg) 9

Chapter Two 11
Penitence, Persuasion and Power: A Performative Model of Confession
    Freedom from Captivity 13
    Problems of Genre: Confessional Literature vis-à-vis Autobiography 14
    The Power of Interlocution and the Relations of Power 15
    Confessional Texts 16
    Rhetoric, Gestures and Emotion 16
    Heteroglossia and Speech Act Theory 18
    The Interlocutor 20
    Power: Hegemony and the Panopticon 21
    From Blindness to Sight: The Symbolic Journey 23
    Auricular and Ocular Confession: A New Confessional Model 24

Chapter Three 27
Confession and Liberty: *Cervantes'* "La historia del cautivo"

Chapter Four 37
Impious and Unbelieving Priests in the Spanish Confessional Tradition
    Epistolary Confession and the Inquisition: Gutiérrez's *Cornelia Bororquia* 37
    The Good but Unbelieving Priest: Unamuno's *San Manuel Bueno, mártir* 40
    The Impious Confessor: Sender's Réquiem por un campesino español 46

Chapter Five 51
"Es de Lope": The Drama of Confession and *Fuente Ovejuna*

Chapter Six   65
Confessing Incognito: Zorrilla's *Traidor, inconfeso y mártir*

Chapter Seven   73
Confessional Literature: Redefining a Genre

Notes   77

Bibliography   83

About the Author   89

Preface

During the writing of this book I have periodically reread Carmen Martín Gaite's statement that "writing without personal delight will never delight anyone" / "nunca lo escrito sin personal deleite puede llegar a deleitar a nadie" (Martín Gaite, *La búsqueda de interlocutor* 24). I hope that the personal delight I have experienced so often while writing this study may be felt by my readers. This book has been one for which I have felt considerable enthusiasm. It reflects not only my interest in confessional literature, but also my passion for the Spanish language and my fascination with the works of Spanish literature that I have analyzed.

Donald Gene Pace
Lexington, South Carolina
January 2009

Acknowledgments

I gratefully acknowledge the helpful assistance I have received from Dr. Ana Rueda. Her suggestions have been most helpful. The counsel, kindness and friendship of Dr. Aníbal A. Biglieri are also deeply appreciated. To Dr. Susan Larson, whose editorial assistance has been helpful, also I express my gratitude. Dr. Gretchen Starr-Lebeau's insights as an historian have enriched this book in significant ways.

Chapter Five is based, with few modifications, on my previously published article "'Es de Lope': The Drama of Confession and *Fuente Ovejuna*," *Bulletin of the Comediantes* 60.1 (2008): 31-50. I express a special thanks to Dr. Edward Friedman (editor) and others who made exceptionally helpful comments.

Our children have been most supportive. My love and thanks go to Joseph, Julia, Rachel, Levi, Camilla, Gene, Rebekah, Wilson, Sarah, William, Robert, Heidi, James, Thomas, and Ann. Camilla and Sarah have been particularly helpful with editorial assistance. The family has patiently adapted to new surroundings and friends following our move to the Lexington, Kentucky area, and then to another Lexington, in South Carolina. My deepest thanks and affection go to my wife Deone. This book is our shared dream.

Chapter One

Liberating a Captive Genre: Past Insights and New Perspectives

The voluminous writing about confessional literature to date has typically categorized it as a subcategory of autobiography.[1] Because confessional accounts often are autobiographical, this labeling is understandable. However, the genre has been unduly restricted by critical classification that has placed blinders upon readers who recognize confessional literature *only* as autobiography. Confession, a genre of liberation, needs to be free itself from conceptual restrictions that precondition readers to overlook confessional elements in many literary works. As Susan M. Levin reminds us, an understanding of confessional literature is important because it provides an additional lens through which to view literary texts, and "[g]enre definition can often lead to a revelation of neglected works" (*The Art of Confession: A Study of Romantic Confessional Writing in France and England* 2).[2]

Despite the many variations of confessional literature, certain conventions typify the genre. Whether religious or secular, confessants share personal information with a confessor-interlocutor. Confession is a ritualistic and rhetorical activity that aims to persuade the confessor while simultaneously helping the confessant in a pilgrimage of self-discovery. Through ritual, a penitent seeks wholeness with self and community. Finally, confession involves a quest for personal freedom, including liberation from bondage, guilt or anguish.

Establishing the Confessional Subject

To establish the theoretical underpinnings of confessional literature, it is imperative to consider three writers who are commonly regarded as authors of confessional classics: St. Augustine, Santa Teresa de Jesús and Jean-Jacques Rousseau. It is also critical to examine twentieth-century Spanish writers (Rosa Chacel and María Zambrano) and theorists (Peter M. Axthelm, Terrence Doody, Dennis A. Foster, Susan M. Levin, Jerry Root, John R. Rosenberg and Thomas Tentler) who have looked closely at the confessional genre.

St. Augustine

Widely regarded as the definitive literary confession is that of St. Augustine (354-430 A.D.) Son of a pagan father and a pious Catholic mother, Augustine eventually becomes Bishop of Hippo, but not before living a less than exemplary life that later brings pangs of guilt. Intensely sensitive, and determined to reveal all to God (the divine interlocutor-confessor to whom his *Confessions* are directed), Augustine confesses both past sins and his newly found faith not only to God, but also to his human reading audience (230): "do I confess, not only in your presence but to men also by these writings, what I now am, not what once I was?" (231). His troubled conscience seeks peace through a reformed life coupled with the public admission of a variety of past moral offenses, a declaration of guilt packed with impressive detail by a man of prodigious memory.

To the future saint, the confessional ritual is a means of liberation from a "prison," of cleansing those who vow allegiance to God's will, of bringing wholeness through sacrifice. Augustine reveals that miraculous divine intervention has broken his bonds and granted deliverance: "the enemy had control of my will, and out of it he fashioned a chain and fettered me with it" (188). He confesses his apostasy to the Manichaeans, who deny the expiatory role of Christ and characterizes his return to Catholicism as a movement from darkness to light (90). He assumes responsibility for his own "will," accepts baptism and confesses that the "inmost physician" (230) has healed his spiritual wounds. This rhetoric of illness regarding "the cure of a guilty conscience" (Tentler, *Sin and Confession* 13) underscores his dependence on an *external* source for *internal* healing, the need for a powerful interlocutor who not only listens but cures.

Augustine's *Confessions* publicizes his performative role as an infirm actor in search of internal wholeness. This transformation is mediated by both Jesus, who supplies grace, and by his own mother, who makes possible both physical birth and spiritual rebirth (see Book 9, 205-28). Augustine, employing a journey motif, yearns to help his "fellow pilgrims," those "fellow citizens in that eternal Jerusalem which [God's] pilgrim people sigh after from their setting forth even to their return" (228). The Bishop of Hippo trusts that the pilgrimage will help him in his quest of self-discovery (233).

Augustine's narrative is exceptionally rich in its treatment of numerous themes that have been identified by critics of confessional literature: the resolution of personal crisis, the issue of revealing all to both divine and human addressees, the oral and written confessional traditions, the question of sincerity, the quest for absolution and moral wholeness, the cleansing role of deity, the relationship between sacrifice and pilgrimage, the balance between human and divine wills, the content of confession, the motivating power of death, the miracle of transformative rebirth, the confessor's complementary roles of healing physician and reproving judge, the discovery of truth about oneself and others, the use of perlocutionary rhetoric, the struggle between evil and good, and the blindness-vision dichotomy. With good reason, the *Confessions* of the Bishop of Hippo has become a standard confession in world literature.

Santa Teresa de Jesús

Recent assessments of Teresa de Jesús' autobiographical book (*Libro de la vida*) call into question its traditional place as a classic Spanish autobiography. Elizabeth Rhodes argues that it is not a confession at all, but simply a "book" (85). Chacel does not regard it as a great confessional text (12). There is general agreement that her text represents a compliant written response to ecclesiastical superiors.[3] What other motives may mask her "confession" is a subject of greater controversy. Jodi Bilinkoff, for example, argues that "this instrument of clerical surveillance also gave women an unparalleled opportunity for self-expression, providing them with the convenient explanation that they were merely writing out of obedience" ("Confessors, Penitents, and the Construction of Identities in Early Modern Avila" 93). Rhodes argues that there may never have been a "Santa" Teresa were it not for the pseudo confession that emerges as a result of her suspicious superiors: "Had Teresa of Ávila responded to her confessors with an autobiography, we would not have her text today" (Rhodes 94).

Like a thesis that endows her with ecclesiastical credentials, Teresa's "Book" frees her to pursue the reforming activities that were much closer to her heart than the writing of a forced "Book": "Only by locating her self deeply within Catholic monasticism could this remarkable woman hope to reform it" (Rhodes 105). Her "Book" is central to her "struggle for credibility" (Rhodes 87). In the two decades after writing her "Book," Teresa launches an impressive number of reforms as she helps establish and direct monasteries, pursuits that likely would have been unlikely without the spiritual credentials acquired from writing her "confession."

Jean-Jacques Rousseau

Speaking of his *Confessions* (published posthumously in 1781), Jean Jacques Rousseau (1712-1778) "decided to make it a work unique and unparalleled in its truthfulness, so that for once at least the world might behold a man as he was within" (478). His *Confessions* demonstrates that no confession is fully transparent, regardless of how determined an author is to make it so. He begins by addressing his confession to God, but his eye seems focused on mortal interlocutors, the reading public, most specifically his posthumous readers (373, 479). As a confession of private thoughts and actions, Rousseau's classic seems to be a genuine effort to portray himself without a mask: "I did not embark on my *Confessions* in order to be silent about my stupidities" (502). Rousseau looks to the readers of his autobiographical narrative for understanding. They are his addressees, the confessors to whom he looks for sympathy and absolution.

The French author fathers five children by Thérèse Le Vasseur, and, to his later regret, gives up each to a foundling hospital (333). He remains true to his strange initial promise to her: "I declared in advance that I would never abandon her, nor ever marry her" (310). While he never abandons her, Rousseau is unfaithful to her, which he confesses directly to her. Thérèse, assuming the role of confessor, first notes Rousseau's "confusion, that [he] had something on [his] mind" *before* hearing his verbal confession: "I relieved myself of my guilty conscience by a free and frank confession" (331). She quickly forgives him, like a priest granting absolution to a remorseful penitent. This episode demonstrates how a minor confessional scene may appear within a work's larger confessional framework. Rousseau's text is thoroughly confessional, both in its overall structure and in embedded confessional scenes.

Rousseau's account, firmly within the autobiographical tradition, serves as a secular counterpart to Augustine's earlier work. It typifies the manner in which confessions are born of crisis, serve as a conduit of self-discovery, are most valid when open and unforced, need not be primarily religious, and express personal emotions. Most importantly, his frank exposition demonstrates that even a sincere and detailed confession is still incomplete, contains subjective biases, and betrays a masked author, even if the mask is unintentional and invisible to the writer. He claims to expose his own life and thoughts, but seems preoccupied with confessing the transgressions of others for whom he feels animosity.

The Theorists' Legacy (Root, Tentler)

The contributions of theorists have helped us recognize and appreciate the various literary genres, including confession. Root and Levin demonstrate that confession extends beyond the formal religious ritual. Zambrano establishes the importance of crises as catalysts that produce confessional narratives. Axthelm underscores the importance of the confessional hero and the role of confession in self-discovery. Chacel argues that a work may comprise the confession of its author. Doody emphasizes that confession, however private, is a social activity. Foster demonstrates that confession has a social context and is a perlocutionary activity that seeks to elicit a response from an interlocutor. Rosenberg elucidates the connection between confession and the cyclical pattern of demise and renewal by which the old person is transformed into the new.

Beyond Guilt and Religious Confession (Root, Tentler)

Jerry Root's *"Space to speke": The Confessional Subject in Medieval Literature* (1997) and Thomas Tentler's *Sin and Confession on the Eve of the Reformation* (1977) stress the importance of the Fourth Lateran Council of the Roman Catholic Church (1215), which made annual confession mandatory, and argues that this ecclesiastical decision not only changed ritualistic religious practices but also medieval literature (Root 1; Tentler, *Sin and Confession* 70). As a spin-off of the Council's determination, technical how-to-confess manuals emerged and confession came to be an important feature in literature. Root provides interpretive analyses of two pre-Fourth Lateran Council confessional writings, by Augustine and Peter Abelard, but his primary focus is on fourteenth century confessions, particularly those of Geoffrey Chaucer, Guillaume de Machaut and Juan Ruiz, author of *Libro de Buen Amor*. He notes that the divergence between the intent of the manuals and the actual statements of the Archpriest in *Libro de Buen Amor* results in "comic results, but it also confirms that the discourse of confession can be taken outside of the institutional framework of the sacraments" (12). Tentler dates the establishment of "[a] formal system of forgiveness of serious sins and reconciliation with the body of the faithful" to the second century, which formed the basis for the severe and totally public canonical penance that prevailed well into the mid seventh century (*Sin and Confession* 4). Meanwhile, in Ireland, an alternate penitential system emerged by the late sixth century that laid the foundations for the private confessional and penitential practices that characterized the High Middle Ages. Greater standardization evolved as clerics relied on brief manuals (penitentials) to know what penance should prescribed for the various sins committed by their parishioners (Tentler, *Sin and Confession* 9).

Tentler summarizes the four traditional elements that have historically characterized the penitential ritual: penitents feel remorse for deviating from religious norms, confess their wayward behavior, submit to some type of penitential performance, and obtain a comforting response from "priests who pronounce penitents absolved from sin or reconciled with the communion of believers" (*Sin and Confession* 3). Conventional reliance on authorized clergy in the confessional ritual is founded on belief in "the power of the keys, a power entrusted to priests by which they could apply the passion of Christ" (Tentler, *Sin and Confession* 65). The link between priestly keys and spiritual healing is heavily rooted in ancient Christian tradition: "[t]he image of the priest as a physician of souls ... originates in the Gospels and is prominent in the Church Fathers and the early medieval penitentials" (Tentler, *Sin and Confession* 157). Tentler concludes that "[t]he greatest promise is that confession is the place of healing" (*Sin and Confession* 158) and emphasizes the connection between psychological well-being and the confessional ritual (*Sin and Confession* 347).

Root maintains that confession may emerge in numerous non-ecclesiastical settings: "the hospital and medical treatment, the marketplace, courts of law, inquisitional trials, and surely other domains less easy to document" (92). Confession, which cannot be "confined to the ear of the priest or the door of the church" (13), has been viewed both as a means of bringing solace to the penitent and facilitating hegemonic authority over congregations (48): "Confession represents an exercise in institutional control, but in order for it to work the Church must cede a certain degree of its authority. It must create and enfranchise its subjects, it must give them a space to speak" (87), and, one might add, space to write and perform. Confession may be a sacred *or* a secular sacrament, a performative ritual directed by clerics believed to hold ecclesiastical keys *or* by lay individuals who made no claim to possessing such authority.[4]

A Genre of Crisis: From Humiliation to Hope (Zambrano, S. M. Levin)

Perhaps the finest critical work on the confessional genre written in the Spanish language is María Zambrano, *La Confesión: Género literario* (1943).[5] According to this writer and critic, the life that seeks after truth is at the heart of this genre that "se ha esforzado por mostrar el camino en que la vida se acerca a la verdad" (24). Ultimate truth, she argues, is always superior to the life of the confessant (16). Confession, "un género de crisis" (24), is necessary when a gap exists between one's life and transcendent truth. Like Zambrano, S. M. Levin argues that confession and human difficulties are closely intertwined. Typically "a specific problem" (26) triggers a confessional account, which helps resolve challenges: "Confession is a means of dealing with troublesome matters that must be faced" (S. M. Levin 244).

Zambrano theorizes that literary genres, including confession, exist because humans feel compelled to express themselves, and that literary genres differ in their response to life's demands (25). Poetry is one such response, history another, and the novel yet another (25). Zambrano recognizes Saint Augustine's foundational role in the confessional genre, but (unlike most other critics) also recognizes the much earlier example of the biblical Job. A true confession, like the account of what Job *said*, carries a continuing sense of immediacy and relevance for the reader: "Toda confesión es hablada, es una larga conversación" (Zambrano 26). Zambrano's beautifully crafted text has the tone of a confession itself, and conveys her deep concern for the despair and humiliation that individuals in the modern world suffer (21, 36). She perceives confession as an academic subject infused with vital contemporary relevance.

Zambrano maintains that the anguished written accounts of confessants spring from crises (32). Confessions are needed to find oneself when weighed down by failure, when humiliated: "cuando el hombre ha sido demasiado humillado, cuando se ha cerrado en el rencor, cuando sólo siente sobre sí 'el peso de la existencia', necesita entonces que su propia vida se le revele" (29, 32). Confession fulfills dual purposes of escape and coping: "la huida de sí" and "[el] buscar algo que le sostenga y aclare" (32). This despair may result from feelings of guilt, but even more fundamentally it is, like Job's anguished confession, "queja, simple queja" (33).

The confessional complaint is infused with hope, for it would not be uttered without confidence in the existence of "un interlocutor posible" (Zambrano 35). Confession reveals an inner conversion that helps one confront fundamental challenges and brings longed for wholeness (35-7). It is thus a genre of *both* angst and hope, escape and renaissance: "huída de sí en espera de hallarse" (37). For Zambrano, confession extends beyond the admission of guilt or revelation of secrets; it is a hopeful activity that involves self-discovery (38), a narrative process that mediates between the death of the old person and the birth of the new.

The Confessional Hero and the Quest for Self-discovery (Axthelm)

In *The Modern Confessional Novel* (1967), Peter Axthelm concentrates on the quest for "reconstructed order" in "a disintegrated world" (54, 97). In this theorist, the confessional hero prefers "self-laceration" to "external rebellion" (9), possesses a "huge capacity for suffering" (9). Axthelm emphasizes the painful isolation felt by confessional figures: "Every confessional hero is essentially alone when he makes his confession"; others who form part of the confessional scene, including judges and priests, "serve only as conventions" (62). This loneliness is reinforced by the oppressive sites in which confessions often occur: "a cell, an underground hole, or a dark city" (9). The confessional hero sometimes "tells his story to another character in a setting reminiscent of the religious confession" (9). To Axthelm, confession involves a "burning quest for self-discovery" (53). S. M. Levin, too, argues that self-discovery is fundamental to confession (13, 14). Each of the twelve confessional texts she examines "all show a person in the process of discovery and setting forth what he is as an individual" (11). Such self-knowledge is particularly important in romantic confessional accounts because their narrators are commonly not only outcasts, but outcasts who are fatherless (11).

The Author as Confessant (Chacel)

In *La confesión* (1971), Chacel advances a conviction, routinely overlooked by critics, that the *Quixote* is an important piece of Spanish confessional literature: "yo considero que Cervantes es el único que nos dio una verdadera, auténtica y pura confesión" (Chacel 9). Chacel's analysis focuses more on the author than on his characters: "Insisto en que el Quijote es *confesión* de Cervantes" (Chacel 44). She reminds us that author and protagonist share a common world (16). Through the fictional don Quijote, Cervantes laughs at himself and confesses his own inner self (46-7). To Chacel, the *Quixote* is a penitential act of its author (49-50). Cervantes confesses to being a defenseless sacrifice to a cruel and bewildering world (51). In addition, through Cervantes' *Quijote*, Spain confesses its internal reality to the rest of the world (55).

The Appeal to an Audience: Confession and Society (Doody)

Terrence Doody's major theoretical contribution to the understanding of confessional literature is his emphasis on the relationship between confessant and community. In *Confession and Community in the Novel* (1980), he argues that the two "are mutually dependent" and that "the need to explain ourselves regardless of the difficulties" finds its counterpart in the "need to hear each other's explanations" (196). Doody's theoretical exploration of the role of community in confession applies equally well to the religious penitent or the secular rebel; each seeks oneness with community (7, 185-86). Both religious and secular penitents confess their deviance from societal norms, acknowledge the right of others to discipline them, and long for reunification. Confession, ultimately a social activity, consists not only of "the deliberate, self-conscious attempt of an individual to identify himself" but also of the revealing of one's self to the audience with which he seeks communion (185).

The role of an interlocutor in confession is well recognized in critical circles, but Doody's contention that the interlocutor provides community has not been as clearly articulated elsewhere as in *Confession and Community in the Novel*. The confessant—who feels a "sense of disconnection (22)—is, of necessity, the creator of the literary confessor with whom he interacts: "the reader of a written confession becomes a confessor, and the nature of his reading is thereby changed" (4). The confessional author often looks beyond the institution or family as confessional interlocutor (as with Teresa de Jesús and Cornelia Bororquia) and imagines an audience of confessor-readers because "no available institution, no system or myth, no class structure, profession, locale, or family quite accommodates" the unique individuality of the confessant (22).

A Perlocutionary Ritual: The Search for Reaffirmation and Healing (Foster)

Confession, according to Foster in *Confession and Complicity in Narrative* (1987), generally "involves a narrator disclosing a secret knowledge to another, as a speaker to a listener, writer to reader, confessor to confessor" (2). By providing a thorough disclosure to an interlocutor, the confessant expects the active interaction of the confessor. Theirs is a symbiotic relationship, not a unidirectional expression (2). To Foster, a defining feature of confessional accounts is "that they are narrated by characters consumed with guilt and driven to talk about it" (18). Foster seeks to narrow the distance between confessional speaker and listener: "The listener is also only human, also a sinner" (3). The confession may be an attempt at individual redemption and purification but it also has a theatrical aspect to it that seeks to share *private* experience with others: "The confession is a 'sacrifice,' a ritual performance, a statement whose purpose is not to represent some event but to enact a relationship between God and man" (20). This complex cultural phenomenon—"a mode by which people enter into the discourse of their culture" (7)—is not performed in a cultural vacuum; confession always has a cultural context. Foster urges us to broaden our definition of confessional expression (7). After referring to texts not generally regarded as confessional, Foster underscores the need for an amplified characterization of the genre: "None of these texts is traditionally confessional, but that is part of my point. The confessional tradition informs the workings of many kinds of narrative" (18).

The Pattern of Death and Rebirth (Rosenberg)

One of the most important recent contributions to the criticism of confessional literature is Rosenberg's *The Circular Pilgrimage: An Anatomy of Confessional Autobiography in Spain* (1994). Drawing on ancient imagery, this author characterizes confession as a bridge between death and rebirth, and demonstrates how this motif has strong foundational links to sacred and secular literary traditions. One of Rosenberg's key theoretical arguments is that "the confessant is a pilgrim who, though moving constantly toward his or her destination, never achieves a sense of having arrived at Jerusalem" (172). The search for personal wholeness, he argues, is fundamental to the confessional literary experience; yet such wholeness can only be approximated, never attained.

This book owes much to the interpretations of the authors and critics whose works have been summarized in this chapter. Their ideas are enlightening and useful. This study is an attempt to build on the collective critical heritage they have crafted by introducing two major theoretical perspectives that have consistently been overlooked: the performance nature of confession, and the incorrect classification of confession as *only* a subset of autobiography. As subsequent chapters demonstrate, confession is not always autobiographical but is always performative.

Chapter Two

Penitence, Persuasion and Power: A Performative Model of Confession

The new theory of confession introduced in this chapter builds on the models of other theorists. It argues that confession need not be relegated to any particular genre, that it may be either religious or secular and that it is ceremonial in nature. It stresses the importance of the interlocutor in the complex interactive game of confession. The model demonstrates how classical rhetoric, speech act theory, hegemony theory and Mikhail Bakhtin's theory of heteroglossia all help explain how confession is a performative ritual aimed at gaining freedom from oppressive personal crises. The model stresses the importance of imagery concerning the eyes and vision and maintains that confession is an activity that is *seen* as well as *heard*.

Whether religious or secular, confession assumes a structure that imitates the Roman Catholic religious sacrament of penance. It involves at least one confessant-penitent who confesses to at least one confessor-interlocutor that typically has superior status and power than the confessant, and seeks to remain the leading actor in a hegemonic relationship. Confession, a type of speech act, is a performative ritual rooted in classical rhetoric that comprises a complex of utterances, gestures and emotions that always have extra-linguistic roots, in accordance with Bakhtin's theory of heteroglossia. It is a two-way communicative process that mirrors Martín Gaite's weaving image: "'dame hilo toma hilo'" (*Retahílas* 96).

For all their theoretical contributions to the study of confessional literature, previous writers have not gone far enough in emphasizing the performative nature of confessional rituals enacted by and in literature. Theorists have correctly highlighted the religious origins of confession, stressed the causational role of crises, recognized the link between penitence and community, identified self-discovery as a key component, acknowledged the importance of the interlocutor, and accentuated the birth-death motif. Each of these aspects of confession relates to rhetoric, including its performative aspects. The performative part of confessional rhetoric falls under the category of *pronuciatio* or *actio(n)*, terms which emphasize the importance of both voice and gestures. According to Quintilian, "Cicero in one passage calls *action* a 'sort of language,' and in another 'a kind of eloquence of the body.' None the less, he divides *action* into two elements, voice and movement, and these are also the elements of *pronuciatio*. So we are free to use both names indifferently" (Quintilian V: 85, 87). Applied to the confessional ritual, *pronuciatio* is a "sort of language" that includes the voice as well as the "eloquence of the body."

The model proposed here, and subsequently illustrated with examples from Spanish literature, demonstrates how an awareness of the hitherto untapped area of confessional performance enriches and complements the theoretical contributions of earlier writers. In so doing, this book expands the focus of confession beyond the written versus verbal paradigm to encompass theatrical considerations as well. Issues regarding human persuasion (perlocution) figure prominently in the field of rhetoric and in speech act theory. The concepts of hegemony (as enunciated by Gramsci and further developed by Foucault) and heteroglossia[1] (as theorized by Bakhtin) inform both approaches. This book draws on each of these areas and proposes a new theory of confession that focuses on power, persuasion and performance.

The sixteenth-century rhetorician Thomas Wilson describes *gesture* as "a certaine comely moderation of the countenance, and al other parts of mans bodie, aptly agreeing to those things which are spoken" (*The Arte of Rhetorique* 220-1). The spoken word should match the emotions and gestures: "That if we shal speake in a pleasaunt matter, it is meete that the looke also should bee cherefull, and all the gesture stirring thereafter" (220-1). Although complete descriptions of the gestures accompanying verbal confession may be absent, the considerations about rhetoric mentioned by Wilson merit consideration. He speaks of the position of the head, the appearance of the forehead and brows, the blowing of the nose, the appearance of the eyes and lips, and the "grenning" of the teeth. He urges consideration of whether "the armes [are] cast abroad [or] comely set out, as time and cause shall best require," as well as the position of the hands: "the handes sometimes opened, and sometimes holden together, the fingers pointing" (220-1). Wilson speaks of "the breast laied out, and the whole bodie stirring altogether, with a seemely moderation" and then summarizes the profound rhetorical impact that bodily gestures can achieve: "By the which behaviour of our bodie after such a sorte, we shall . . . preswade [others of] the trueth of our cause" (Wilson 220-1).

By applying Wilson's rhetorical instructions to a hypothetical confessional scene, one can envision a penitent communicating with a confessor by bowing the head, wrinkling the forehead, drawing the brows together and blowing the nose, while tears fill the eyes, lips quiver and teeth do no "grenning." Motions of the arms support verbal statements, while the hands and fingers are clasped in a pleading gesture. Meanwhile, the breast reflects the confessant's distressed sighs and sobs, all in an attempt to persuade the priest as to "the trueth of [one's] cause" (Wilson 220-1). The penitent, and the confessor, must be *seen* as well as *heard*.

Consideration of the theatrical aspects of confession (including words, actions, emotions and gestures) dovetails nicely with the moral pilgrimage theme that is common in confessional literature. Whether a moral pilgrimage, an idealistic quest, or a sacrificial journey aimed at personal purification, such activities are inherently theatrical. Of course, the theater holds no monopoly on dramatic enactment. Poetry, novels, and short stories also exploit dramatic gesture and performance.

The title of a study of confession by Peter Brooks, *Troubling Confessions: Speaking Guilt in Law and Literature* (2000), reveals the common perception of confession as a *verbal* activity. One might appropriately add that in both law and literature guilt is not only *spoken* and *written* but also *performed*. This performative interpretation of confession is complemented by speech act theory, and by Bakhtin's theory of living heteroglossia, which emphasizes extra-linguistic content. Confession is theatrical; it involves actors who may play their roles with the utmost sincerity, or dramatically feign what they do not personally feel. Masks are fundamental to the *dramatis personae* on the confessional stage.[2]

Freedom from Captivity

Confessional literature is an ancient form of writing that consists of accounts of confessional activity—whether written, verbal or theatrical—that may be private or public, individual or collective. It involves a confessant who seeks freedom and a confessor-interlocutor (explicit or implicit) to whom the confessant looks for liberty. The Old Testament account of Job, an early example of confession, centers on the penitent's desire to gain freedom from his intense sufferings. Although rooted in religious tradition, a confession may be religious, secular, or both (as in the case of the Inquisition, which is both religious and political). It typically involves significant personal transformation associated with a quest for liberty. This search for freedom through confession assumes many forms. In religious confessions the penitent, burdened by pangs of conscience or some other affliction, searches for relief. In a political confession, the secular penitent may seek freedom from his secular *confessors*, who also have power to liberate. The classical tension between justice and mercy is fundamental to these crises. The voluntary quest for deliverance, for mercy from God, may involve a far different "pilgrimage" than a quest for mercy from a repressive regime. Whether in a religious or secular setting, the confessant typically seeks to be liberated from the penalties of justice and seeks someone with authority or power who can grant religious absolution or secular liberation.

Although the loss of freedom (including imprisonment or exile) appears frequently in confessional literature, it is a theme that has not been examined adequately. Those seeking relief from torture are often induced to confess. Those facing imminent death, due to illness or execution, tend to feel an unusually strong desire to reveal their inner selves, to recount the transformation they have experienced to an interlocutor-confessor. Some confessants recount their liberation from false ideas or write to clear their consciences; they use the confessional genre as a rhetorical instrument to push social agendas or to persuade others to adopt their ideological outlook.

Confessions often effect and reflect a profound ethical transformation of an individual, as in the case of Augustine. Although an account of personal transformation need not be framed within a good versus evil paradigm, all genuine confessants view the new person as superior to the old. Consequently, confessions routinely have a retrospective time factor that other genres do not characteristically possess. Reflecting back on one's former self allows the confessant either to reveal a genuine transformation or to mask a nonexistent change. Ethical arrogance is common in confessants, which leads them not only to praise their new life but, by implication, to condemn those who continue to wander in error. The religious convert has a conversion story to tell that denigrates an earlier way of life; the political zealot cannot resist telling why other political outlooks are flawed.

Problems of Genre: Confessional Literature vis-à-vis Autobiography

Confessional accounts may be autobiographical or biographical, true or fictional. The confessional genre may overlap with other literary forms, but it is not automatically subservient to autobiography, or any other genre. Zambrano theorizes that literary genres exist because human life feels compelled to express itself, and that which distinguishes one genre from another is its particular response to life's demands: "Lo que diferencia a los géneros literarios unos de otros, es la necesidad de la vida que les ha dado origen" (25). A confessional work may be fictional or historical, a short story or a novel, poetry or prose, autobiography or biography, but what all have in common is the sense of crisis and the search for liberation that inspires a confessional account. It has commonly been assumed that confessional texts are a subset of the autobiographical genre, but one may just as well, and just as inaccurately, argue that autobiographical texts are a subset of the confessional genre. Not every autobiography is confessional nor is every confession an autobiography. While both autobiography and confession could exist in a literary world devoid of the other, each is enriched by the other's presence. Confessional texts share common features with other types of literature, particularly with other genres of intimacy, such as letters, diaries, journals, and autobiographies.

An entire work need not be *confessional* in order to merit consideration as an example of the genre. Although this book concentrates on texts that have an overall confessional frame, it also emphasizes the importance of limited confessional incidents within those works. Such confessional scenes may also exist in works that lack a global confessional frame, but our interpretation of such works is enriched by learning to recognize and appreciate even minor confessional situations. The *Quixote*, for example, is not typically considered to be confessional literature, and yet one can make the case that it is a profoundly confessional text, both in its overall structure and in many specific episodes. Likewise, novels such as *La familia de Pascual Duarte* and *Réquiem por un campesino español*, and dramas such as *Fuente Ovejuna* and *Sueño de la razón* combine confessional frames with embedded penitential scenes. To be alert to such possibilities, even in well-known texts, invites a new reading that permits us to reconsider them as part of the confessional tradition, and allows us to appreciate how the genre of Augustine, Teresa and Rousseau is also that of Cervantes, Lope, Unamuno, Buero, Sender and others.

The Power of Interlocution and the Relations of Power

Because of Spain's Catholic heritage, which places heavy emphasis on the confessional ritual, Spanish writers are predisposed to utilize confessional frames and refer to penitential scenes. Confessional rhetoric is part of their personal worlds as well as those they create in their narratives and dramas. Moreover, because of their familiarity with the conventions surrounding the religious sacrament of penance, Spanish readers easily identify with these scenes. Besides the religious underpinnings of Spanish confessional literature, one must take into account the historical settings of both authors and their texts. Power relationships are inherent in confessional scenes, which are influenced by country's dominant institutions, including the Inquisition and political regimes. Although this book spotlights Spanish literature, the theoretical perspective upon which it relies can just as well be applied to the confessional literature of other languages and places. This study privileges a *type* of literature over specific authors or historical periods.

Without an interlocutor, there is no confession. Just as each narration presupposes the existence of both a narrator and a narratee (Gerald Prince, "Introduction to the Study of the Narratee" 190, 200), so the existence of a confessant presupposes an addressee-confessor. Moreover, the narratee, or interlocutor (as theorized by Carmen Martín Gaite in *La búsqueda de interlocutor y otras búsquedas*) shapes the content of the work. This interlocutor may be visible or invisible, present or future, human or nonhuman, historical or fictional. As Prince asserts, "the narratee ... is a necessary feature of any model of narrative" ("The Narratee Revisited" 299). This authorized interlocutor need not be a recognized ecclesiastical official, but must have power to bring the penitent back into favor with a larger community (John L. Tofanelli, "The Gothic Confessional: Language and Subjectivity in the Gothic Novel, *Villette*, and *Bleak House*" 7). Both the Protestant Reformation and the Catholic Counter-Reformation allowed greater individualism, which in turn led to a proliferation of settings in which the human inclination to confess was satisfied (Tofanelli 12).[3]

The role of the narratee is linked to another important theoretical concept: hegemony. As theorized by Antonio Gramsci (*Prison Notebooks*), Michel Foucault (*Discipline and Punish*) and others, hegemony involves an examination of power relationships between individuals, and between individuals and institutions. Power and institutions are intrinsically linked to confession. There is, for instance, a hegemonic relationship between confessant and confessor (which may be a friend, a cleric, or a repressive regime), a relationship that involves not only *control* but also *consent*. Interlocutors (including confessors), and the institutions and regimes they represent, exert control in various ways, but ultimately that control is strongest when the confessant's consent cements a hegemonic relationship. Interlocutors and confessants mutually influence each other and attempt to shift the balance of power in their own direction.

Confessional Texts

This book focuses primarily on novels and dramas to explicate how the new theory of confession applies to specific literary works. It examines Miguel de Cervantes' *Don Quijote* as a personal and national confession, Luis Gutiérrez's *Cornelia* Bororquia as a confession related to the Inquisition, and Miguel de Unamuno's *San Manuel Bueno, mártir* and Ramón Sender's *Réquiem por un campesino español* as examples of unbelieving or guilty priests. Theatrical performance, including its kinesthetic aspects, also forms part of the confessional genre. Lope de Vega's *Fuente Ovejuna* illustrates the theme of collective penitence; José Zorrilla's *Traidor, inconfeso y mártir* portrays the link between confession and self-discovery; while the short plays of three contemporary dramatists (Lidia Falcón O'Neill, and Salvador Enríquez) demonstrate how confessional literature can promote various social agendas.

Rhetoric, Gestures and Emotion

Quintilian writes that when the great orator "Demosthenes was asked what was the most important thing in the whole business of oratory, he gave the prize to Delivery, and he gave it the second and the third place too" (Quintilian V: 87, 89). As the Roman rhetorician clearly understood and explained, verbal communication is not only verbal, but also performative. When confessions are given or described in literature, it is imperative to take notice of non-written and non-verbal communication. This agrees with modern theories of linguistic meaning, such as that of William P. Alston, who emphasizes the importance not only of what speakers *say* but also what they *do* while speaking: "it will always be true that the speaker is doing something" (*Philosophy of Language* 32). Speech in general, and confessional speech in particular, is part of a performance that exceeds mere words.

Whether in the courtroom or the confessional, gestures and the emotions they inspire in others are essential to rhetoric, the art of persuasion. In fact, when gestures contradict spoken words, it is the gestures that carry the greater rhetorical weight. Rhetoric, as Paul Ricoeur reminds us, "has always been defined as a strategy of discourse aiming at persuading and pleasing" ("The Metaphorical Process as Cognition, Imagination, and Feeling" 432). Confessants seek to do the same; they attempt to please and persuade the confessor. In their role as confessional judges, priests grant absolution after they are persuaded by the speech acts, the words and emotional appeals, of their penitents. The clergy may also utter their own perlocutionary statements designed to sway their parishioners to transform themselves. In both cases, emotion is part of the confessional interchange. As Quintilian observes: "Proofs may lead the judges to *think* our Cause the better one, but it is our emotional appeals that make them also *want* it to be so; and what they want, they also believe" (III: 47). Thus, to keep emotional appeals before a confessor vibrant and effective, both verbal and nonverbal action is needed: "Again, all emotions inevitably languish, unless they are kindled into flame by voice, face, and the bearing of virtually the whole body" (Quintilian V: 87).

Confessants may be regarded as actors in a private setting, and gestures—"expressive tool[s] for the actor" (MacDonald Critchley, *Silent Language* 221)—help to facilitate the sharing of intimate thoughts in a ritualistic setting. Confessional gestures are part of a "symbol-system" and have roots that derive from religious ritual. Part of the confessor's task is to interpret both verbal and non-verbal signs: "gesture, though silent, is full of eloquence to the vigilant and sagacious onlooker who, holding the key to its interpretation, knows how and what to observe" (Critchley 221). Such is the task of one who hears, and sees, confession.

In confessional settings, as in the innumerable scenes of daily life, "the face is sovereign" where gestures are concerned. Both confessor and penitent can learn much from the face of the other, because it "makes us understand many things [and] often replaces words altogether" (Quintilian V: 123). Martín Gaite, who refers to the face as a "segundo texto" (*El cuento de nunca acabar* 25), also reminds us that facial gestures can belie what the mouth is saying (379). According to the ancient master of rhetoric Quintilian, the eyes are the supreme facial feature, and the eyebrows also communicate much (V: 125). In terms of persuasive potential, the eyes have a unique rhetorical companion: the capacity to weep (Quintilian V: 125, 134). Jacques Derrida reminds us that even the blind can weep (*Memoirs of the Blind* 126-7). In confessional communication, the eyes, eyebrows, and tears of both confessant *and* confessant are important. Martín Gaite suggests the powerful communicative role of the eyes when she says that "cada mirada incuba una historia" (*Retahílas* 97). The eyes of both confessants and confessors can reveal pent up knowledge, betray innermost sentiments, and not only weep but cry out.

Quintilian argues that personal character, independent of what one says and does, is an important part of rhetoric: "And surely the best man to persuade others . . . will be the man who has previously persuaded himself" (Quintilian V: 211). Whether in a religious or secular setting, confession is a reconciliatory ritual: "The power to conciliate comes generally either from acceptability of character (which shines through somehow also in the voice and the Delivery) or from charm of style" (V: 165). "I am not only saying that the orator must be a good man," Quintilian contends, "but that *no one* can be an orator *unless* he is a good man" (V: 199). The most genuine confessants wear the thinnest masks.

Heteroglossia and Speech Act Theory

Bakhtin's notion of "heteroglossia"—which Hazard Adams and Leroy Searle define as "those conditions, the converging of internal and external forces, that control the meaning of an utterance" (*Critical Theory Since 1965*, 667 note 7)[4]—serves as a useful theoretical concept because it helps to explain the complexity of even seemingly simple confessional utterances. Viewed through the prism of heteroglossia, "Fuente Ovejuna did it"—a Spanish town's famous confessional admission—is not merely a simple linguistic statement but representative of a complex set of political, cultural, religious, and social inferences. This statement, as well as every other confessional utterance, comprises a vital part of what the Russian theorist terms "living heteroglossia" (Bakhtin, *Discourse in the Modern Novel* 668). Heteroglossia is an overarching theoretical umbrella that covers all aspects of confessional literature.

Heteroglossia theory dovetails nicely with speech act theory, an approach that dates back to John L. Austin's *How to Do Things with Words* (1962). Published posthumously, it would be others, such as John Searle and H. P. Grice, who would develop the theory Austin proposed (M. H. Abrams, "Speech Act Theory"). Wolfgang Iser argues that speech acts "are linguistic utterances in a given situation or context, and it is through this context that they take on their meaning" ("The Repertoire" 361). This book advances a "confessional speech act theory," which, like speech act theory generally, "attempts to explain exactly what happens when human beings speak [or confess] to each other" (Jeremy Hawthorne, "Speech Act Theory"). It examines what power relationships are involved and, in the tradition of classical rhetoric, the theory stresses the importance of evaluating confessional utterances in context. Where, for instance, does a confession take place? Are the participants kneeling, sitting, or standing? Is coercion involved or is their uninhibited volition? How does the meaning of words take on performative meaning? What ritualistic conventions are followed by penitents and confessors? (Hawthorne, "Speech Act Theory"). The words "I do" take on different performative meanings when spoken in a wedding ceremony than at a ball game in which the question is asked, "Who has a good view?" "I am guilty" has far graver meaning when said in a courtroom (or confessional) than it does in a restaurant as a response to an accidentally spilled drink.

Confessional dialogue often involves what Searle labels "indirect speech acts," complex expressions that are, for example, ironic or metaphoric (*Expression and Meaning* 30). In confessional expression, a statement of culpability may also double as a request for absolution or a plea for social change. What is said at the personal level ("I confess") may also be an indirect admission of national guilt ("We confess"). "I have sinned" carries the indirect or implied meaning of "I desire absolution." Such indirect speech acts are only understood when both locutors draw "on their mutually shared background information, both linguistic and nonlinguistic" (Searle *Expression and Meaning* 31-2).

Even literal significance is typically linked to extralinguistic factors (Searle *Expression and Meaning* 117). The "literal meaning" of a penitent's statement, for instance, is contingent upon such rhetorical factors as location, emotion, gestures, purpose and the degree to which conventions are followed. The same words may mean different things if said meekly by a kneeling penitent with head bowed or proudly by a fist-shaking confessant who remains standing. There is more meaning in a typical confession than meets the *eye*, or the *ear*. Without context, speech is merely a sequence of sounds.

According to speech act theory, "statements not only *are* things, but they typically *do* things" (Hawthorne, "Speech Act Theory"). The word "absolution," when spoken in response to the confession of a penitent, not only *is* an expression but *does* something to the confessant. The basic building blocks of language meaning are what Daniel Vanderveken and John R. Searle call "illocutionary acts" (Vanderveken, "Universal Grammar and Speech Act Theory" 25; John R. Searle *Expression and Meaning: Studies in the Theory of Speech Acts* 7, 18). When people make simple statements, they *perform* "elementary illocutionary acts such as assertions, questions, orders, declarations and thanks" (25). By participating in conversations, they intentionally join with others to perform "*collective illocutionary acts* such as exchanging greetings" (Vanderveken, "Universal Grammar" 25).

Institutions and practices help to shape the meaning of illocutionary speech acts. Confession may have a far different meaning in a cathedral than in a court room. In harmony with Bakhtin, Searle argues that "[t]here are a large number of illocutionary acts that require an extra-linguistic institution," such as ecclesiastical, governmental or political organizations (*Expression and Meaning* 7, 18). A religious confessional ritual, or its secular variations, is dependent on such an extra-linguistic institution, without which the confessor would lose authority, credibility, or both. This may occur when both penitent and priest (or the secular counterpart) each has a special relationship with regard to an institution (Searle, *Expression and Meaning* 18).

Not only are extra-linguistic institutions important but also the goals that speakers try to achieve through their interaction. Speakers interact verbally with "in order to coordinate intelligently non verbal actions such as cleaning the house" (Daniel Vanderveken and Susumu Kubo, "Introduction," *Essays in Speech Act Theory* 18-19). The confessional ritual involves human interaction in support of goals that extend far beyond simply holding a conversation, getting better acquainted, or sharing information. Confessors and confessants participate in a dialogue "in order to coordinate intelligently non verbal actions," such as clearing an individual conscience or preserving social order. Extra-linguistic purposes are fundamental to the confessional ritual.

The speech act, in general, is classified as illocutionary. If such an act also has the secondary effect of persuading, convincing, or otherwise exerting an effect on a hearer that exceeds a mere comprehension of the spoken word, then the illocutionary act doubles as one that is perlocutionary (John R. Searle, Ferenc Kiefer and Manfred Bierwisch, eds., "Introduction" *Speech Act Theory and Pragmatics* vii; Steven Davis, "Perlocutions" 54). Perlocutionary speech acts have a discernible impact on the hearer, as when causing fear, inspiring confidence, or securing loyalty (Abrams, "Speech Act Theory"; J. L. Austin 838). An *illocutionary* confessional performance that induces another to feel hopeful or to accelerate personal transformation moves beyond the *illocutionary* to the *perlocutionary* (Hawthorne, "Speech Act Theory").

Conventions are vital to confession (Hawthorne, "Convention"). One common convention requires the penitent to *kneel* before a confessor who *sits*. Deferential language and gestures, and respect for authority are other typical conventions. These types of socially-constructed conventions are "artificial" (Hawthorne, "Convention") practices that are reinforced by standardization and institutionalization. Without rules and conventions, confession cannot function. While capable of substantial variation, the confessional ritual, like the performance of illocutionary acts, is founded on conventions and is "a rule-governed form of behaviour" (Searle "What Is a Speech Act" 61).

Understanding the mental state of the participants in a confessional interaction is essential to fully understand the speech acts that are taking place. A penitent may silently kneel to say "I feel humble," weep to convey "I am sorry," or nod the head to indicate "yes" (Bernard Moulin and Daniel Rousseau, "An Approach for Modelling and Simulating Conversations" *177).* Observers, including confessor, confessants, and readers, may interpret such acts as if they were speech. Still, they may be misled because they lack "access to the locutors' mental models" which help "to decide which linguistic or non-linguistic actions they will perform" (Moulin and Rousseau 177). Kneeling may, after all, be superficial, tears feigned, and a nod of the head insincere. Confession is a complex game in which each actor gauges and seeks to shape the mental state of the other principal actor(s). Emotions, gestures, and words all provide hints about the beliefs, biases, intentions, sincerity and flexibility of the actors in a penitential performance ("An Approach" 184).

The Interlocutor

Carmen Martín Gaite—a novelist and theorist of the importance of communication—is impressed with Unamuno's contention that he could not speak "'si no veo unos ojos que me miran y no siento detrás de ellos un espíritu que me atiende'" (*Cuento* 155). So it is with confession, whether written, verbal, performed, or any combination of these modes. There is always an interlocutor, whether seen or unseen, whether heard or unheard. Penitents speak to someone and hear someone, albeit with an inner voice (*Cuento* 155-7). The human desire to hear and be heard is met, in part, by confessional communication. Quoting a great eighteenth-century intellectual, Martín Gaite makes a thoughtful observation regarding the role of the confessional interlocutor: "'La elocuencia—escribió el Padre Sarmiento—no está en el que habla, sino en el que oye'" (*Búsqueda* 20). Without the confessor-interlocutor, not only would all the words, emotions and gestures of a penitent be in vain, but they might never even come into being: "si el interlocutor adecuado no aparece en el momento adecuado, la narración hablada no se da" (*Búsqueda* 20). To have the active participation of the interlocutor (including the confessor-interlocutor), and not merely the functional presence, ensures a healthier rebirth of the penitent: "eso es lo fundamental, que no se te vaya el interlocutor, que no se te duerma" (*Retahílas* 96). The Jesuit Paolo Segneri, author of a popular manual for confessors, argued in 1685 that the most important approach a confessor could take was simply to listen (Brooks 99).

Perhaps the finest imagery to illustrate this point is the weaving metaphor that Martín Gaite employs to describe the interactive nature of one-on-one communication. While reflecting on the individualized role of the interlocutor in *Retahílas*, she makes an observation that describes the ideal artistic interaction between penitent and confessor: "el que oye, sí, ése es quien cataliza las historias, basta con que sepa escuchar bien, se tejen entre los dos, 'dame hilo toma hilo'" (*Retahílas* 96). This give-and-take relationship, this giving a thread and taking a thread, is central to the interchange of speech acts in confession. As Ana Rueda notes, the interlocutor functions as a "nudo mágico de comunicación" ("Nudos de interlocución" 306). To understand the confessional genre, one must give serious emphasis to *both* confessant and confessor.

Power: Hegemony and the Panopticon

Confessional speech act theory is strengthened by adding a heavy emphasis on power, as theorized by Foucault. Both speech act theory and rhetoric are concerned with human persuasion, and a related theory of influence that informs these two approaches is hegemony theory. Popularized by Marxists, and used widely by others as well, hegemony theory seeks to explain why subjected individuals or groups submit to control when not forced to do so (Hawthorne, "Hegemony"). Although not universally applicable to the analysis of confessional scenes—especially where violence, or the threat of violence, removes human volition—hegemony theory provides a theoretical construct from which to examine confessional literature. A confessant may be subject to the hegemonic power of a religious confessor, whose office, prestige, and institutional authority make even a difficult confession seem personally desirable.

The hegemonic power of the confessor may be used as a means of bringing order to individual lives and to communities. The "first principle [or confession] was the sacramentally ordained priest's dominance, which was expressed in a variety of ways" (Tentler, *Sin and Confession* 345). Such dominance by a church or a political entity invites or requires the subservient *consent* of those whom they seek to *control*. As accepted mediators between God in heaven and penitents on earth, the clergy are positioned to exercise the type of *control* that elicits the voluntary, self-interested *consent* of their ecclesiastical subordinates. Penitents confess because they perceive some personal benefit in participating in the confessional ritual: "Only priests could absolve from serious sin—with the words 'I absolve you' [a perlocutionary act]—and place the penitent in contact with the passion and merits of Christ" (Tentler, *Sin and Confession* 345). Brooks argues that confessional probing by a cleric and interrogation by a law enforcement officer are similar activities in which priests and "police interrogators appear to share an understanding that the bond of confessant and confessor often is crucial to the production of confession" (35). To secure the true cooperation of the confessant requires perlocutionary rhetoric that leaves human volition intact.

The hegemony of confession is most likely to be achieved when the confessor is a skilled interlocutor who allows, and even encourages, the penitent to talk freely and discover why a transformation is personally desirable. Like a doctor seeking to bring hidden disease into the light, the confessor's probing involves both speech and silence. This communicative process parallels the revelatory process by which hidden disease becomes a protagonist that comes to light: "the whole dark underside of disease came to light, at the same time illuminating and eliminating itself like night, in the deep, visible, solid, enclosed, but accessible space of the human body" (Foucault, *Birth of the Clinic* 195). *Illumination* of disease, whether physical or moral, is thus linked to *elimination* of the infirmity.

When confessional authority becomes abusive or relies on violence to coerce, hegemony cannot be as fully achieved because voluntary participation is partially or totally inhibited. In analyzing such cases, the notion of the "panopticon" becomes particularly important as a theoretical tool, as demonstrated by Foucault's study *Discipline and Punish* (1975). Jeremy Bentham invented the term to express an architectural idea. To improve vigilance in a prison and other institutions, Bentham advocated the utility of a central tower in a location from which all prisoners could be monitored: "[a]ll that is needed, then, is to place a supervisor in a central tower and to shut up in each cell a madman, a patient, a condemned man, a worker or a schoolboy" (*Discipline and Punish* 200). Founded on what Thomas R. Flynn calls "the marriage of power and visibility," the panopticon is a flexible concept that can be applied to a variety of institutions for purposes that are either benign or oppressive ("Foucault and the Eclipse of Vision" 279).

Foucault explains that Bentham's concept has awakened substantial interest because of its flexibility and adaptability, and argues that this idea not only relates to the control of prisoners but also to the creation of "the carceral city" and "the disciplinary individual" (*Discipline and Punish* 308). In dealing with tyrannical political or religious leadership, the panopticon has much more to do with process than architecture; it is not only a "dream building" but "a way of defining power relations" (*Discipline and Punish* 205) in situations in which there is "a gross imbalance of power" (Alfred Arteaga, "An Other Tongue" 15). Individual penitents, like Foucault's "disciplinary individual," may become subject to the panoptic *gaze* of confessor-observers, and to the ideological out*look* of powerful institutions.

Foucault speaks of the panoptic power that religious organizations possess via their "centres of observation disseminated throughout society" (*Discipline and Punish* 212). The multiplicity of confessional sites provides a manner in which a Church, political regime or other powerful institution can, for good or ill, (1) classify its subordinates, (2) discipline those that do not share their own discursive vision, and (3) attempt to establish an atmosphere in which each person fears potential punishments deriving from the vigilance of those situated in panoptic "towers" (*Discipline and Punish* 195, 204-5, 220, 305; Flynn 280; Robert T. Spires, *Post-Totalitarian Spanish Fiction* 40).

From Blindness to Sight: The Symbolic Journey

Although traditionally perceived as an oral ritual—as reflected by the term in "auricular confession"—the visual component of confession must not be overlooked. The blindness-sight metaphor, a form of bondage-liberation imagery, is important in confessional literature. The network of confessors, like a panoptic web seeking both to assist penitents and protect society, represents the converted and healed, societal midwives who see clearly and are empowered to mediate the transformation of others. The gaze of their eyes represents power and vision. The confessants, who hide their eyes in shame and avoid the gaze of their robed hearers, seek conversion and healing, and look to the clergy to help them remove their blindness and experience a personal metamorphosis. They act, believing they are seen by the eyes of others with greater power than their own, including the all-seeing eye of Providence, the penetrating vision of a repressive monarch, or the monitoring gaze of the local priest. They seek, through confessional rhetoric, to extract absolution from those on whose power they rely for absolution. With roots stretching into antiquity, the blindness-sight dichotomy has deep roots in classical literature and the confessional ritual, which involves seeing the gestures of another, looking inwardly, thinking (seeing) correctly, and visually assessing one's interlocutor.[5] Both literally and metaphorically, confession is both an ocular and an auricular ritual. The confessor, is not limited to *hearing* confession, but may also *see* confession. Confessional rhetoric is intimately tied to light and sound, to the eye and the ear, to visible gestures and audible speech. Images involving light or sight are particularly important because liberation from personal crisis in a common theme in the confessional genre. To escape from darkness or blindness is an important symbolic journey that confessants seek. Derrida speaks of the "theme of guilty blindness" (*Acts of Religion* 209), a topic with important metaphorical relevance to confession. Not to open one's eyes to truth is tantamount to what Hans Blumenberg calls "the willful and culpable shutting of the eye" ("Light as a Metaphor for Truth: At the Preliminary Stage of Philosophical Concept Formation" 45) to avoid viewing what one should see. To refuse an offer (or a command, as in *Fuente Ovejuna*) to confess to one in authority likewise constitutes eye-shutting rejection of personal or institutional authority; it represents lack of vision.

A classic religious narrative involving blindness-sight-conversion imagery is the New Testament account of Saul-Paul. After persecuting believers, Saul sees a heavenly light, hears a divine accusatory voice, and is smitten with blindness. After traveling (like a pilgrim) to Damascus and going three days without food or water, a believer named Ananias restores his physical sight, which parallels his acquisition of spiritual vision (KJV Acts, Chapters 8-9). The correlation between confession, light and conversion is also prominent in Augustine's *Confessions*. The Bishop of Hippo views his divine Confessor as the supreme Physician who has power to heal his wounds and grant him clearer vision (Augustine 168). In the tradition of Augustine, Blumenberg writes of "the inner *illuminatio*" that accompanies the contemplative closing of the eyes (Blumenberg 45). Confessing to God that "the house of [his] soul . . . contains things that offend your eyes," he pleads with his divine interlocutor to cleanse that house (Augustine 46). The cleansing role and vision of the interlocutor are here laid down as a model for earthly confessors who simultaneously strive to cleanse individual houses and purify the collective house of the Church. Concerned over his own "house," which is struggling through its mortal pilgrimage, he yearns to move toward God's "house, which is not on pilgrimage" (Augustine 46, 312).

In describing his symbolic journey toward greater vision, Augustine perceives the unity between light, truth, and healing: "you will light my lamp, O Lord my God, you will enlighten my darkness" (Augustine 109, based on Psalm 17:29). He yearns for certainty about things unseen, desires spiritual healing, and seeks greater vision in order to find truth: "By believing I could have been healed, so that my mind's clearer sight would be directed in some way to your truth" (Augustine 138). Concerned for his "soul's health" (138), he realizes that he must believe to be healed: "In truth, it [his soul] could never be healed except by believing" (138).

Auricular and Ocular Confession: A New Confessional Model

The new theoretical synthesis proposed in this chapter complements earlier models by focusing on the performative aspects of confession. It concedes that confessional literature is commonly autobiographical but argues that it is not limited to that genre. Whether religious or secular, the confessional ritual imitates the religious sacrament in which at least one confessant-penitent and one confessor-interlocutor attempt to interpret and respond to the other. The new theory recognizes the reality of collective confession as well as the more common individual variety. All parties are affected by the speech acts of all other participants. Confession is a liberty-seeking rhetorical ritual in which perlocutionary speech acts—including utterances, gestures, and emotions—are employed in order to persuade others.

The proposed model recognizes the importance of written and verbal aspects of confession but moves the theoretical debate into the realm of performance. Drawing on Bakhtin's notion of heteroglossia, it stresses the importance of analyzing non-linguistic content, including cultural factors and the role of institutions. Confessors often represent institutions, which empower them to carry out a midwife role by providing mediation to those who seek freedom in the form of absolution, comfort, or other types of liberation from crises. The power of these confessors enables them to exert hegemonic influence over their penitents, who consent to this control because of the benefits they expect to receive. Confession is not only heard but seen. Consequently, eyes and images concerning vision are important in the ritual. Eyes seek or avoid visual contact and reflect the power relationships in confessional encounters. Imagery relating to blindness and vision also figures prominently in confessional literature; vision, light, conversion, transformation, and freedom all relate to this motif. The following chapters illustrate ways in which this new model of power, persuasion, and performance applies to specific works of Spanish confessional literature.

Chapter Three

Confession and Liberty: *Cervantes'* "La historia del cautivo"

Confessional writing may overlap autobiography but it is not automatically subservient. Until the eighteenth century, genres were limited to four classical categories: comedy, epic, satire and tragedy. Since that time, greater flexibility has been the norm and other categories have been added, including biography, essay, novel and short story (Cuddon, "Genre"; Abrams, "Genre"). A genre may be viewed as "a set of constitutive conventions and codes, altering from age to age, but shared by a kind of implicit contract between writer and reader." Modern writers and critics recognize the nonexclusivity of genres and acknowledge significant overlap among them (Abrams, "Genre"). Zambrano views genres as varied reactions to the challenges of human life (25). Autobiographies may result from the desire of individuals to tell their personal stories for any number of different reasons. These first-person accounts may or may not refer to crises, but not so with confession, "un género de crisis" (Zambrano 24). Confessional literary frames and embedded confessional scenes, regardless of how secular, typically imitate the religious sacrament of penance, a sacrament aimed at resolving personal crises.

Miguel de Cervantes' *Don Quijote de la Mancha* is, among so many things, a confessional novel with a confessional frame as well as many embedded confessional scenes.[1] While much of the *Quijote* is told from a third-person perspective, "La historia del cautivo" is an autobiographical narrative that serves as a multilayered confession, one that may be read as the novelesque autobiographical confession of Cervantes.[2] Like the complete novel, "La historia del cautivo" (*DQ*, Part I, Chapters 37-41) has a confessional frame that is enriched by confessional episodes. Through his confessional narrative, the protagonist, Ruy Pérez de Viedma, not only reveals secret knowledge to a listening audience that serves as a collective confessor-interlocutor but also, as with confession generally, comes to better understand himself (Sieber 129). Without this audience there would be no confession. Although we learn his name, in the narrative he refers to himself as *el cautivo*, which privileges his role as Christian hostage over his individual identity. In his tale of Christian deliverance from Islamic captivity, he is the "conductor" (307), a Moses figure who leads Zoraida and others to the promised land of Spain.

Embedded in "La historia del cautivo" is don Quijote's "dissertation" on arms and letters that doubles as a profession of his religious belief and strengthens the religious tone of *el cautivo*'s confession. He extols the value of "las divinas, que tienen por blanco llevar y encaminar las almas al cielo" (409) and argues that military pursuits are superior to a literary vocation because military arms "tienen por objeto y fin la paz, que es el mayor bien que los hombres pueden desear en esta vida" (409). He waxes eloquent as he quotes the words sung by angelic messengers, "Gloria sea en las Alturas, y paz en la tierra a los hombres de buena voluntad". He cites Jesus' teachings on peace: "Mi paz os doy; mi paz os dejo" (409). These references relate to the theme of discovering religious truth that is prominent in the confessional activity in the story.

Following the scene in which don Quijote confuses wine bags for giants, and "slays" them by spilling their "blood,"[3] an individual called *el cautivo* (Ruy Pérez de Viedma) appears in the presence of Dorotea, Luscinda, Don Fernando, and don Quijote. Accompanying this escaped Christian slave is Zoraida, a beautiful woman dressed in Moorish garb who is seated upon an ass. She does not speak Spanish, only Arabic, but in spite of this barrier to communication, the small group with don Quijote is intrigued by her and her companion and presses to discover who they are, what they believe and what their activities have been.

As the theory of heteroglossia argues, an examination of the utterances of individuals is inadequate without a careful consideration of non-linguistic factors that provide meaning for those utterances. We can understand Dorotea and Luscinda's interrogation of Zoraida, and the narrative of *el cautivo*, much better by realizing that theirs is a Mediterranean world drenched in religious symbolism and rivalry, a society obsessed with questions of cultural conformity. Dorotea prods *el cautivo* to reveal whether his Moorish companion is a Christian, basing her suspicion not on what anyone has said, but on "el traje y el silencio" (406). *El cautivo* admits that her dress and person are indeed Moorish, but insists that her soul longs to be Christian: "tiene grandísimos deseos de serlo" (406).

Assuming the role of joint confessor with Dorotea, Luscinda picks up the inquisitorial thread and concludes that she has never been baptized. *El cautivo* persists in his attempts to calm their fears by countering that she remains unbaptized due to lack of opportunity to receive this sacrament because she has just left Algiers, her native land (406). He then asserts that "Dios será servido que presto se bautice con la decencia que la calidad de su persona merece, que es más de lo que muestra su hábito y el mío" (407) Consistent with speech act theory, not only *el cautivo*'s words convey meaning but also other kinesthetic acts, their non-Christian dress and her silence; their manner of dress "muestra." In this scene Dorotea and Luscinda mimic the role of a male ordained confessor, while *el cautivo* serves as a proxy for the penitent Zoraida, whose dress masks her innermost beliefs. This camouflage of her deepest convictions and true identity are symbolized by the veil she wears. The removal of this veil reveals the exceptional beauty of the *la mora* and suggests her willingness to abandon an Islamic practice that clashes with the expectations of her Christian audience.

When the couple first arrives, Dorotea urges Zoraida not to be distressed by the lack of accommodations, arguing that this problem is very common. Zoraida's silent response—"no respondió nada" (406)—is accompanied by gestures indicating her gratitude. Luscinda, Dorotea, and the other women assume that her silence unquestionably proves that she is a "mora," because "no sabía hablar cristiano" (406). The women thus categorize the Spanish language as Christian, while implying that Arabic, the great language of Islam, is pagan. Zoraida's silence signifies much more to these parochial Christian women than the mere absence of words; it is an indirect speech act that betokens her disbelief in the Christian religion they espouse.

The communication between the couple and their audience introduces the issue of the death of the old person and rebirth of the new, so important in Christian and confessional literature. When Don Fernando asks Ruy Pérez de Viedma the name of his companion, he responds "lela Zoraida" (407).[4] Hearing her name spoken, she eagerly implores that the old (Islamic) name be replaced by her new (Christian) name, María. Her Christian identity is further reinforced by the fact that there is no room for her and her Joseph-like companion in Juan Palomeque's inn (405).[5] Zoraida's proclivity to wear costly jewelry—"más perlas pendían de su hermosísimo cuello, orejas y cabeza que cabellos tenía en la cabeza" (437)—conforms to beliefs regarding the Virgin that were common at the time of Cervantes.[6] The confessional speech act by which "la más hermosa mujer de la Berbería" (432) proclaims her new name has powerful perlocutionary effect. It symbolizes the death of her Islamic past and the birth of her Christian future: "Estas palabras y el grande efecto con que la mora las dijo hicieron derramar más de una lágrima a algunos de los que la escucharon, especialmente a las mujeres, que de su naturaleza son tiernas y compasivas" (407). Pleased with María's abandonment of her Islamic past, Luscinda gives the Moorish Christian an affectionate embrace and states, "Sí, sí, María, María" (407).

The narrative of *el cautivo* is much more than an individual confession; it is a national confession that proclaims the superiority of the Spanish nation while advancing a subtle appeal for greater catholicity in terms of accepting minority groups. The three principal confessants—*el cautivo*, Zoraida-María and Morrenago (*el renegado*)—seem to personify the universal appeal of Roman Catholicism. Ruy Pérez de Viedma is an Old Christian (Sieber 122), María is a convert from a Moorish household and *el renegado* is a lapsed Christian seeking to return to his religious roots. Each confesses individually, and yet their combined speech acts produce a collective confession that suggests the universal attraction of Christianity and its superiority over Islam. The individual confessions are thus symbolic of larger religious patterns and comprise the national confession of a people for whom Christian-Islamic tension is a sensitive and acute challenge. "La historia del cautivo" is noticeably biased against Islam, as seen in Zoraida's warning to *el cautivo*: "no te fíes de ningún moro, porque son todos marfuces [deceitful]" (430) and in *el cautivo*'s assertion that "las moras no se dejan ver de ningún moro ni turco, si no es que su marido o su padre se lo manden. De cristianos cautivos se dejen tratar y comunicar, aun más de aquello que sería razonable" (436). Zoraida writes to *el cautivo* that Christians "cumplen lo que prometen mejor que los moros" (431) "La historia del cautivo" recounts how Moors capture, imprison, and enslave Christians while Christians promote liberty and truth.

The narration of *el cautivo* is prompted by Don Fernando who, like a confessor, prods his confessant to reveal information that otherwise would remain secret; in response. After Ruy Pérez consents to obey Don Fernando's entreaty, others echo his request: "El cura y todos los demás se lo agradecieron, y de nuevo se lo rogaron" (414). Although a clergyman plays a role in urging the confessional statement, it is a collective interlocutor-confessor that presses its enigmatic guest to divulge what he has hitherto kept private.

Cervantes' confessional tale is rendered more meaningful when considered—following the theory of heteroglossia—in the light of prevailing social attitudes, national pride, and religious and ethnic biases. Both author and protagonist address an audience from a fervently Christian nation that has a long-standing hatred and distrust of the Moors. By placing much of the confessional drama in Northern Africa, Cervantes allows *el cautivo* to introduce the reader to non-European life and customs while both reaffirming and criticizing Spanish religious traditions. While the narrative clearly favors the Christian worldview, it also points out flaws in that perspective. As Sieber indicates, "[dishonesty] is attributed to Moors, Turks, renegades and Christian captives alike" (122). Cervantes recognizes the multicultural nature of his society and pleads for less national and religious parochialism. Zoraida herself functions as "a frontier, a borderline between the Christian and the Muslim worlds" (María Antonia Garcés, *Cervantes in Algiers: A Captive's Tale* 204). In a written confession to Ruy Pérez de Viedma, Zoraida mentions both Lela Marién and Alá—the revered Virgin Mary and the Islamic God—in a single sentence (430). *El cautivo* and his future wife blend their Christian verbal professions with the clothing worn in Islamic communities, a performative representation of amalgamated cultures and religious traditions. Even the language in which captives and their superiors typically communicate is a fusion of Arabic and Spanish. When *el cautivo* first meets Zoraida's father, Agi Morato, they communicate "en lengua que en toda la Berbería, y aun en Constantinopla, se halla entre cautivos y moros, que ni es morisca, ni castellana, ni de otra nación alguna, sino una mezcla de todas las lenguas, con la cual todos nos entendemos" (436-7).

Zoraida personifies a combining of cultures. Not only does she profess a change in her religious identify by assuming the name of the Virgin but she also plays the role of mediator for her future husband and other captive Christians who escape with them. As *el renegado* tells Zoraida's Agi Morato about his daughter, "ella es cristiana, y es la que ha sido la lima de nuestras cadenas y la libertad de nuestro cautiverio" (445). Chains symbolize the Moorish penchant for imposing captivity on Christians, while Zoraida's filing off these fetters typifies the Christian penchant for liberty. *El renegado* stresses the importance of free choice in adopting Christianity and insists that "ella va aquí de su voluntad" (445). Zoraida thus personifies important confessional metaphors; she is "como el que sale de las tinieblas a la luz, de la muerte a la vida y de la pena a la Gloria" (445). Concerned about his daughter's apostasy from Islam, the aged Agi Morato assumes the role of confessor himself as he bluntly interrogates Zoraida, insisting that she confess the truth regarding her religious sentiments. To his query, "¿Es verdad lo que éste dice, hija?", she admits "Así es" (445).

Ironically, Zoraida's Christian confession and participation in an escape attempt from her father's garden inadvertently transforms her father from a free man to a captive of Christians. He asks his daughter about her conversion: "¿Que, en efeto—replicó el viejo—,tú eres cristiana, ya la que ha puesto a su padre en poder de sus enemigos?" (445). Zoraida confesses, "La que es cristiana, yo soy" (445) but denies having intentionally reduced her father to bondage, claiming that her only intent is to care for her own welfare. When asked by her Moorish confessor-father what she has done to further her wellbeing, she advises him to present his query to the Virgin Mary, Lela Marién, "que ella te lo sabrá decir mejor que . . . yo" (445). Her father then impulsively dives into the sea to end his life but is rescued by those on the ship (445-6). In this episode, Islam is linked with death and irrationality, while Christianity brings renewed life. Agi Morato emerges from the water in a sort of secular baptism. Later, in a speech act reminiscent of Christian sacerdotal absolution, he cries out to his daughter, "que todo te lo perdono; entrega a esos hombres ese dinero, que ya es suyo" (447).

"La historia del cautivo" is a confessional narrative that features the performative confession of both *el cautivo* and his beloved North African redeemer. It is she who dispenses her father's money to pay the ransom for those who are powerless to free themselves without her miraculous intervention. Garcés argues that "[t]here is no question . . . that money is an obsessive and all-pervading theme in this text" (212). Obviously, money is necessary for ransom—for the fictional Captive Ruy Pérez de Viedma and the historical Captive Miguel de Cervantes. Ruy Pérez refers to the wealthy redeemer Zoraida as the lady who provides liberty (Garcés 215), an "appellation [that] evokes one of the titles given to Mary as the protector of the captives held by the Turks: 'Nuestra

Señora de la Libertad'" (Garcés 215). As a female and a *mora*, Zoraida is an unlikely Christ figure that ransoms Ruy Pérez. Zoraida directs the escape plans from above; from a tiny upstairs window—covered by latticework that hides her from view and is evocative of a confessional—she dispenses both secret messages and enabling financial support. She lowers confessional messages in a white handkerchief fastened to a cane while *el cautivo*, as if gazing toward heaven, see a handkerchief attached to a cane (427). Through gestures and words, she confesses her Christian faith and also her desire to marry *el cautivo* who endures a prisoner's chain, lives in "aquel baño"—"nuestra prisión" (427)—and dreams of being ransomed (322). He also observes another symbol of her piety when she displays from the window "una pequeña cruz hecha de cañas" (428). Her first written message to Ruy Pérez has "al cabo de lo escrito hecha una grande cruz" (429), her personal confession of faith to her Catholic interlocutor. In return, he confesses his own Christian belief through a gesture; after seeing the large cross she had drawn, he recalls, "Besé la cruz" (429).

Not only does Zoraida mediate for him but he, in turn, does so for her. He is her interlocutor, her self-designated confessor and the Christian husband she seeks, but his interaction with Zoraida takes place on her terms. In this relationship, Zoraida chooses to confess when and to whom she pleases. Her money, her beauty and her potential for delivering Ruy Pérez from captivity combine to strengthen her hegemony over *el cautivo*, whether he is acting as confessor or confessant. Having been taught Christianity as a child by a female slave, Zoraida seeks to carry out the pilgrimage-like journey that this woman admonishes her to accomplish; "La cristiana murió, y yo se que no fue al fuego, sino con Alá, porque después la vi dos veces, y me dijo que me fuese a la tierra de cristianos" (430). Zoraida encourages *el cautivo* to respond by gestures if he cannot write back in Arabic, and trusts that Lela Marién will help her interpret his signs. She confides that she often kisses the cross and trusts that the Virgin Mary (Catholic) and Ala (Islam) will jointly preserve him (431).

What next ensues is a confessional interchange in which the two locutors take turns as confessants and addressees as they patiently weave a confessional tapestry in a manner reminiscent of Martín Gaite's prescription for effective interaction: "dame hilo toma hilo" (*Retahílas* 96). As Zoraida proposes in her first letter to Ruy Pérez, "En la caña pondré un hilo: ata allí la respuesta" (430). In the response he sends heavenward to the window of "señora mía" (431), *el cautivo* wishes her the combined protection of "el verdadero Alá . . . y aquella bendita Marién, que es la verdadera madre de Dios," and like a discerning priest, assures her that her desire to travel to the "tierra de cristianos" has been placed in her heart by the Virgin "porque te quiere bien" (431). As he counsels her, *el cautivo* asserts his own conviction that a benevolent Marién instructs those who obediently follow her commands, and that Alá has blessed them with a translator to facilitate their ongoing communication. After promising to marry her after they arrive in Spain, he again invokes divine protection upon his beloved: "Alá y Marién . . . sean en tu guarda, señora mía (431).

The Moorish redeemer's next message to *el cautivo* recommends a plan of escape from her father's garden and provides ransom money. She confesses that although she has diligently pleaded for Lela Marién's assistance to discover how to escape, she has received no answer to her plea (327). She expresses concern that *el cautivo* honor his commitment to marry her and warns that should he fail to do so, "yo pediré a Marién que te castigue" (432-3).

Another important confessional figure in "La historia del cautivo" is the Renegade Morrenago, who confesses his Christian faith and urges others to provide testimonials attesting to his sincerity. He seeks to end his apostasy from the Holy Mother Church and to be restored to the community of believers. Originally from Murcia, he longs to return both to the faith and to land of his birth (429-30). It is he who translates for Zoraida and *el cautivo*. Although he plays a pivotal role in the escape of Ruy Pérez, Zoraida, himself and others, initially he finds it challenging to earn *el cautivo*'s trust. Ruy Pérez is uncertain whether or not to trust any renegade due to the group's dubious reputation for probity. In this case Morrenago seems to have been genuinely converted to Catholicism and sincerely desires to rejoin the community of believers. Renegades are abundant in Algiers during the era depicted by "La historia del cautivo"; they "constituted six thousand of the twelve thousand households counted in Algiers between 1577 and 1581" (Garcés 36). Although these converts to Islam are usually Christian apostates, some are Jewish. For the most part the Christian apostates "were corsairs who dedicated themselves to privateering in the Mediterranean" (Garcés 36). In spite of the initial misgivings of *el cautivo*, *el renegado* comes to be so trusted that at one point in his narrative *el cautivo* remarks, "determinamos de ponernos en las manos de Dios y en las del renegado" (434).

In a confessional scene in which *el cautivo* plays the role of secular confessor, *el renegado* insists that he may be trusted and entreats the group of prospective escapees to confide in him and promises to risk his life for their freedom. To buttress his profession,

> sacó del pecho un crucifijo de metal, y con muchas lágrimas juró por el Dios que aquella imagen representaba, en quien él, aunque pecador y malo, bien y fielmente creía, de guardarnos lealtad y secreto en todo cuanto quisiésemos descubrirle, porque le parecía, y casi adevinaba, que por medio de aquella que aquel papel había escrito había él y todos nosotros de tener libertad, y verse él en lo que tanto deseaba, que era reducirse al gremio de la santa Iglesia, su madre, de quien como miembro podrido estaba dividido y apartado, por su ignorancia y pecado (431).

This confessional speech act—with its words, tears and crucifix—is a performative ritual that illustrates how confession extends beyond the written-versus-spoken paradigm. Non-linguistic content adds to the persuasiveness of *the* verbal utterances of *el renegado*. Both confessant and interlocutors are moved by the scene and *el cautivo* plays a mediating role similar to that which Zoraida effects for him. *El renegado* also plays a mediating role when, as translator and trusted Christian, he assists Zoraida and *el cautivo* in gaining the liberty they seek. To prove his fidelity to others, *el renegado* follows the common practice of acquiring testimonial letters that attest to his integrity (429-30). His rhetoric includes "tantas lágrimas y con muestras de tanto arrepentimiento" (431) that he secures the trust he seeks, and subsequently plays a pivotal role in the captivity to freedom drama depicted in "La historia del cautivo."

As Doody theorizes, confession brings one into harmony with some type of community and so it is with each of the three confessants. Zoraida seeks to be one with a Christian community for the first time, *el cautivo* longs to return to his Christian homeland, and *el renegado* desires to gain readmission to the Church from which he has apostatized. In each case, they seek oneness with the Spanish, rather than the Islamic, community. Their mutually-supporting confessions reinforce the alliance that permits their joint escape.

In the narrative, temporal salvation comes through ransom money provided by Zoraida, who seeks to abandon her Moorish heritage for Christianity. Her confession through the window is accompanied by coins. Moreover, through the costly jewelry she wears, she personifies a wealthy redeemer who personally brings salvation to herself and others. In a religious sense, the term "ransom" has deep ties to Christian doctrines related to confession, sin, penitence, bondage, liberty, atonement, grace, forgiveness, priesthood, and miracles. In "La historia del cautivo," the ransom of Christian captives is associated with a miraculous escape from a garden that is launched—with the assistance of Zoraida, "una deidad del cielo, venida a la tierra para mi gusto y para mi remedio" (438)—on a Friday, which is the day on which Jesus' crucifixion occurred.[7] Pretending to ask for fruit from the garden, *el cautivo* goes to the "jardín de Agi Morato's" (also called the "jardín de Zoraida"; 435-6) to make arrangements for his and others' escape (435-8). Ultimately, Zoraida is the individual who ransoms the Christian captives in an escape that involves twelve Spaniards (436), perhaps symbolic of the twelve apostles of early Christianity.

Ruy Pérez's confession recounts a circular journey that begins and ends in Spain (Sieber 116) and transforms him into a new man. Along the way, he suffers shame, becomes disassociated from his family and home community, faces an uncertain future that seems only to promise perpetual captivity, confesses his inmost beliefs, confides in other Christians for ransom and liberation, and is ultimately reunited with the community of his birth. Having completed his dramatic pilgrimage of self-discovery, this man of arms and letters chooses the confessional genre to reflect aloud on the metamorphosis he has experienced and the liberty he has gained. At another level, the author Cervantes seeks to come to grips with his own identity through this partially autobiographical confessional account, a narrative that extols two dominant aspects of Cervantes' life: arms and letters. Following his military activity at Lepanto, return to Spain, capture by Barbary pirates (Garcés 1),[8] imprisonment in Algiers for five years (1575-1580) and subsequent liberation, Cervantes (like Ruy Pérez) replaces arms with the pen (Sieber 130).

Cervantes' imprisonment proves traumatic and potentially life-threatening for the future author of *Don Quijote*. In a scene narrated by Ruy Pérez, the character "de Saavedra" (427) is introduced. Like his historical counterpart (Miguel de Cervantes de Saavedra), the fictional de Saavedra narrowly avoids death. He escapes impalement, the common Algerian means of inflicting capital punishment; fortunately, his master "jamás le dio palo" (427) In "La historia del cautivo," it is just after de Saavedra survives this scare that Zoraida appears, which makes the captivity-liberation theme particularly striking (Garcés 207, 419). Garcés argues that the ordeal Cervantes undergoes enriches his writing and leads to his emphasis on the captivity-freedom motif: "trauma in Cervantes functions as a fountain of creation" (5). This theme of bondage and liberty, so important in "La historia del cautivo," and in the life of the author Cervantes, is one of the central themes in confessional literature.

"La historia del cautivo" exemplifies the theoretical model presented in this book. It is a framed confessional narrative in which several individual confessions contribute to an overall confessional structure and tone. All confession in this tale occurs outside the confessional and a priest is involved in only a minor way, yet there is a distinctly religious tenor throughout. It contains autobiographical elements that relate to Cervantes' life and reveal personal information about both his and the fictional captive's dramatic circular pilgrimages. Cervantes' narrative constitutes a frontier between fictional and autobiographical confession (Garcés 185-91). "La historia del cautivo" is a confession of Cervantes' determination not to become a renegade himself, his refusal to renounce Christianity for Islam (Garcés 59). His despair at ever being ransomed seems apparent, for he makes four unsuccessful escape attempts (Garcés 38-59) prior to being ransomed (Garcés 106-10) and gaining his freedom. Still he does not opt for the immediate freedom that confession of Islamic belief would grant him. Ruy Pérez, like Cervantes, does not apostatize from Catholicism to gain renegade privileges.

In spite of its strong autobiographical content, there are elements that are not autobiographical. Scenes involving Zoraida's written and verbal confessions are recounted in the third person as are the confessional activities of *el renegado*. Ruy Pérez's story is an example of how confession is a form of rhetoric, the art of persuasion. Confession is a liberty seeking ritual, something that is abundantly illustrated in the narrative of *el cautivo*. Perlocutionary speech acts abound as utterances, gestures, and emotions combine to persuade interlocutors. The rich cultural background that Cervantes includes in his narrative supports Bakhtin's theory of heteroglossia, which stresses the importance of non-linguistic content. The confessions include not only important verbal utterances, but also symbolic gestures, emotional displays, and even figurative objects, such as a white handkerchief, a cane, a cross, and coins which liberate captive Christians. Without the broad interpretative approach suggested by heteroglossia, these confessions may seem mere statements that assist in plot development, and may not even be recognized as confessional in nature or representative of larger religious and national themes.

In "La historia del cautivo," varying configurations of confessants and their interlocutors appear, and all participants are affected by the speech acts of all other confessional actors. Different individuals mediate for others in a complex confessional game in which confessors and confessants assess and react to the perceived mental state of their interlocutors. Confession is both heard and seen, as such images as conversion, blindness, sight, captivity and liberation contribute to a confessional tone that has not been fully appreciated by critics. Finally, "La historia del cautivo" provides an example of an embedded confessional narrative in Cervantes' classic novel, itself a confessional work that includes many hitherto unappreciated confessional scenes.

Chapter Four

Impious and Unbelieving Priests in the Spanish Confessional Tradition

Confessional accounts are varied in their narrative perspectives and are not limited to autobiography. Rhodes argues that texts are categorized by *genre* (an adaptation of *genus,* as used in the natural sciences), and that "this process of classification is bound to collide on occasion with samples the categories cannot accommodate" (Rhodes 79). Such collisions are common in confessional literature. Gutiérrez's *Cornelia Bororquia* is an epistolary novel in which first-person accounts (letters) reveal confessional activity that is not limited to the epistolographers themselves. In Unamuno's *San Manuel Bueno, mártir*, a first-person confessant reveals the confessions of others as well are her own. Sender's *Réquiem por un campesino español* is a third-person confessional novel that contains two parallel confessions, one in prose (by an anonymous narrator) and one in verse (by an altar boy whose recitation of a *romance* is interspersed throughout the novel).

Epistolary Confession and the Inquisition: Gutiérrez's *Cornelia Bororquia*

Luis Gutiérrez lashes out at the Inquisition in his epistolary and confessional novel *Cornelia Bororquia o la víctima de la Inquisición* (1799-1800). Predictably, the Inquisition prohibited his novel, one that raises fundamental questions related to confessional literature. Is the novel, in its entirety, a confessional piece? How does the protagonist's prison experience typify the confessional experience in general? What role does the preservation of one's reputation play in confession? How does Cornelia play the roles of both confessor and confessant? What role does the quest for absolution play in confession? What impact does being faced with imminent death have in motivating an individual to confess. How does the author weave both voluntary and involuntary confession into his narrative?

Each of the protagonist's four letters is written from prison, where she languishes prior to her execution, the unjust result of an unwarranted incarceration instigated by the lustful Archbishop of Seville. As with confessional writing in general, her letters are intensely introspective and reveal personal values, including her passionate zeal to have future generations know that hers was a life of virtue (Carta 32, 166). To her father, she confesses her moral integrity—a quality that ultimately leads her to the flames: "vuestra hija sabe respetar la virtud" (Carta 4, p. 70). The epistolary interchanges that make up the novel strengthen the typical confessional tendency to reveal secret information, privileged knowledge that could not otherwise be known. The work in its entirety exhibits a confessional tone as it reveals, through intimate letters, surprising revelations about the Archbishop. His own end-of-life confession deepens the novel's confessional content (Carta 32, 170). The protagonist's confession emerges most directly in her four letters, numbers 4 and 8 (to her father, the Governor of Seville) and numbers 23 and 32 (to her fiancé Bartolomé Vargas).

In the confessional tradition of Augustine, hers is a sacrificial journey, a moral pilgrimage. Cornelia is "la inocente víctima" (Carta 33, 176) of intolerance and male cruelty: "Yo sufro, pero soy inocente, y esta sola reflexión me consuela y tranquiliza" (Carta 4, 73). Her crisis is externally imposed by a powerful individual and a repressive regime, the Inquisition. Although her confidence in the Archbishop is shattered (Carta 4, 72), she still confesses her religious faith: "Nuestra augusta y sagrada religión" (Carta 4, 73). Given the fundamental role of the bishop in confession (Paul Anciaux, *The Sacrament of Penance* 126), it is highly ironic to have an archbishop-villain. Cornelia is intensely concerned with what future humanity will think of her. She fears that her name, which deserves respect, "será puesto en los templos a par del de los judíos y herejes" (Carta 32, 166). She is troubled by "la triste idea de la infamia" (Carta 32, 166). This concern for personal reputation is a compelling force in her confession and those of other confessional authors. While imprisoned, Cornelia suffers in confessional settings not of her own choosing. She is appalled by the questions of the "Inquisidor General," a spider spinning a web (Carta 8, 86).[1] Her confessor, far from being a source of consolation, "es mi mayor, mi más cruel verdugo" (Carta 32, 165). Her interlocutors, including the novel's readers, sympathize with the confession her evil confessor refuses to accept (Carta 32, 165). With regard to the Archbishop, Cornelia wistfully exclaims, invoking the blindness-vision imagery seen in Augustine and in biblical references, "¡Si quisiera Dios abrir los ojos al viejo Arzobispo, si le dejara conocer sus horrendos delitos!" (Carta 23, 133).

Besides the confessional tone and content of the teenaged protagonist, the novel includes the confession of the primary villain, the Archbishop of Seville. Cornelia confesses to the inquisitor, who questions her claim of "¡Inocencia!" after having killed the Archbishop. She admits to having taken the life of her pursuer, but insists that she acted in defense of her virtue and honor (Carta 32, 170). The inquisitor rejects her claims that the Archbishop was the instigator of her unjust incarceration, and refuses to acknowledge the validity of her allegation that the aged prelate had confessed his guilt to her personally just before expiring. His desperate confession dramatically demonstrates that confession is not simply heard but performed: "El mismo postrado a mis pies, lo ha confesado delante de todo el mundo a la hora de su muerte" (Carta 32, 170).

Neither of the two letters (numbers 21 and 25) in Gutiérrez's epistolary novel from the Archbishop himself is confessional. It is in a letter (Carta 26, 139) from Lucía to Cornelia's fiancé Vargas that we learn of the dying prelate's mournful confession. In an ironic inversion of roles, Cornelia becomes, as it were, his confessor. Following an unsuccessful attempt to persuade Cornelia to sacrifice her virtue to his lust, the two engage in a fight which results in her mortally wounding her oppressor with a knife. Sensing his life ebbing away, the Archbishop desperately confesses, through words and gestures, his culpability: "lleno de remordimiento y próximo a parecer ante el juez supremo, declaró la verdad . . . y arrodillándose como pudo a los pies de doña Cornelia, con una voz triste y trémula" (Carta 26, 139). He confesses having kidnapped Cornelia, instigated the death of her father, and caused Cornelia to suffer in wretched prison conditions (Carta 26, 139). He envisions her as his future judge: "Cuando compareciere al juicio de la majestad terrible, tú, joven infortunada, tú estarás allí para condenarme" (Carta 26, 140). The Archbishop fears divine retribution and conjures up a dramatic post-mortal scene in which Cornelia's father, the Governor of Seville, consigns him to infernal flames (Carta 26, 140). Begging for the mercy he never granted Cornelia—"Perdonadme, hija mía, perdonadme" (Carta 26, 140)—the nineteen-year-old Cornelia mercifully, and theatrically, pardons the elderly ecclesiastic: "cogiéndole de la mano, le levantó con el mayor respeto de sus pies, acordándole generosamente el perdón que solicitaba" (Carta 26, 140).

The Archbishop's dramatic confession is all the more *confessional* because reference to it is embedded within the "Extracto del último interrogatorio que se hizo a Doña Cornelia Bororquia, escrito de su propio puño" (attached to Carta 32). In this legalistic document, apparently a forced *written* confession required by her priestly accusers, she testifies to the Archbishop's dying *verbal* and *performative* confession and openly acknowledges her own *verbal* confession to having killed her tormentor in self-defense.

In spite of her innocence, Cornelia is put to death. In the theatrical confessional scene prior to her execution, she finally receives the privilege of dealing with a just Confessor. At the scaffold, near which a bloodthirsty and insulting crowd has gathered, "La triste doncella . . . levanta los ojos al Cielo y exclama dolorosamente: 'No, no queráis privarme también de este alivio . . . Sí, yo veo al Dios que va a juzgarme: él está a mi lado, sabe mi inocencia, me escucha, y va a recibir en sus manos mi afligido espíritu: vedle allí, vedle allí que viene a mi socorro . . . ¡Dios de bondad! En tus manos, Señor, encomiendo mi alma: amparadme y fortalecedme'" (Carta 33, 176).

Gutiérrez's work shows that confession is an exceptionally rhetorical literary form, one that invites a closer look at its performative dimensions. Although *Cornelia Bororquia* is an epistolary novel, its scenes are dramatic (even melodramatic). The performative nature of its scenes induces the reader to view confession as a performative activity; gestures and emotion, place, and other circumstances enhance words. As the theory of heteroglossia suggests, meaning is significantly enriched by nonverbal content in *Cornelia Bororquia*. This nonlinguistic content includes a tradition of Spanish anticlericalism, a suspicion of priestly exploitation of young females, and a collective awareness of the atrocities of the Inquisition. This understudied novel has never been classified as a confessional work, but as we have seen, it clearly deserves recognition as such.

The Good but Unbelieving Priest: Unamuno's *San Manuel Bueno, mártir*

Gutiérrez's anticlerical novel introduces a recurring theme in Spanish literature: the impious or unbelieving cleric. Because of the personal and confidential nature of the confessional ritual, it is easily subject to skepticism and disparagement, whether merited or not. In the case of Cornelia Bororquia, the confessional authority of the priest is blatantly misused. In Unamuno's *San Manuel Bueno, mártir* (1979) [1930], we see an unusual combination of goodness and unbelief, as well as an unbelieving priest. The epigraph with which the novel begins was written by an earlier saint, the apostle Paul: "Si solo esta vida esperamos en Cristo, somos los más miserables de los hombres todos" (1 Corintios 15:19; *San Manuel Bueno, mártir* 95).[2] In this confessional account, don Manuel serves as priest of Valverde de Lucerna, a village whose name suggests two important images in confessional literature: rebirth (represented by *verde*) and illumination (symbolized by *luz*). Don Manuel is an admired pillar of the community, but is also a pitiful mixture of comedy and tragedy, a blend of unhappy fool and insecure philosopher, a cleric with no faith in the hereafter. He is a dearly beloved heretic who inspires others by outward performances while inwardly rejecting fundamental theological positions.

Don Manuel leads an alternative Church, similar enough to Roman Catholicism not to arouse popular suspicions, yet vitally different. Only his disciples know the truth, and with him they promote the Holy Mother Church of Valverde de Lucerna (*SMBM* 113-14). Its *credo* mimics that of the established Church, but omits the fundamental statement of belief in bodily resurrection (Gregory Peter Andrachuk, "'He That Eateth of This Bread Shall Live Forever' (John 6:58): Lázaro's Communion" 208; Summer M. Greenfield, "La 'iglesia' terrestre de *San Manuel Bueno*" 610). In his congregation, don Manuel initiates the practice of having the entire community join in a collective confession to God. They recite the *Credo* as if with one unified voice, but when they intone the words "creo en la resurrección de la carne y la vida perdurable" (*SMBM* 103-04), their priest remains silent, thus tacitly confessing disbelief in this fundamental Christian doctrine.

Through secret confessions implanted within a confidential manuscript, the web of unauthorized belief is revealed to the reader. The written confession that frames the entire novel is kept secret from ecclesiastical authorities, but inexplicably falls into the hands of Unamuno, the author's namesake who appears in the novel. Confession dominates *San Manuel Bueno, mártir*, and is a medium by which the author Unamuno questions the doctrines of heaven, hell, God, Satan, resurrection, and the practice of beatification. His multilayered confessional novel is a probing meditation on the practice of confession itself.

Although the core of the novel is Ángela Carballino's written confession, it centers on don Manuel, a faithless Christ figure who shepherds his flock by deceiving them, by withholding secret truths from all but select disciples to whom he divulges the truth. Ángela's written confession, which mirrors Unamuno's own, includes confessional episodes involving herself, her brother Lázaro, the fool Blasillo, don Manuel, the priest's deceased father, and all the people of Valverde de Lucerna. She intends to keep her confession beyond the reach of the Church, whose leaders she fears and distrusts. Ángela assists the bishop who is gathering facts in support of the beatification, an attempt to transform *don Manuel* into *san Manuel*, but she refuses to share the enigma of the saint's doubt-based parallel church with the prelate. Her account classifies the bishop's beatification document as incomplete and false and, unlike the bishop's hagiographic account, is the true *promoter fidei*.[3]

Tentler suggests that a confessor is both judge and doctor (*Sin and Confession* 3, 13, 157-8), and although don Manuel helps his penitents "to derive profound psychological benefits from sacramental confession" (Tentler, *Sin and Confession* 347), he does not carry out the judicial functions associated with discipline. When a young unwed mother returns to Valverde de Lucerna, don Manuel finds a man to marry the unfortunate woman and act as a father to her child. A priest with an amoral outlook, he is not as interested in assigning culpability as in providing consolation (*SMBM* 99-100). On another occasion, a judge from a nearby village seeks to enlist the priest's assistance to encourage a bandit to confess his criminal activity. Fearing that the accused will face punishment if he confesses, don Manuel withholds his assistance (102-3). Negligent as a judge, he is superb as a healer, although his curative powers derive from earthly charisma rather than heavenly gifts (100-01).

Ironically, the priest who publicly enacts a duplicitous performative confession is so revered by his flock that "Su acción sobre las gentes era tal que nadie se atrevía a mentir ante él, y todos, sin tener que ir al confesonario, se le confesaban" (102). Part of his ongoing public confessional enactment is to say mass, and everyone in town attends these services as if they were a theatrical event (103). Ángela confesses to don Manuel on a number of occasions, and he, in turn, becomes her penitent; theirs is a symbiotic confessional relationship. At her first confession, a bewildered Ángela initially finds herself speechless, which constitutes a voiceless speech act that conveys her mental state[4] to her priestly interlocutor (111-12). Like a typical confessant, she begins with some postural or emotional gesture, and only later expresses words (Dene Barnett, *The Art of Gesture: The Practices and Principles of Eighteenth Century Acting* 373). When Ángela stammers the prosaic "yo pecadora" (111), it is a continuation of her confession, not its commencement. Don Manuel, more in response to her emotional communication than to her routine words, seeks to calm her. He challenges the source of her fears: "Porque tú no tiemblas ahora al peso de tus pecados ni por temor de Dios, no; tú tiemblas de mí, ¿no es eso?" (*SMBM* 111-12). The confessant's emotional messages exert a perlocutionary effect on the cleric and gain his sympathy and consolation; ultimately, Ángela leaves this first penitential encounter profoundly soothed (112). Ángela's emotional appeals are a nonverbal way of soliciting help. Although her experience is personal, it is also social; it affects herself and her interlocutor: "Emotions thus seek to change outer and inner situations" (Stanley Keleman, *Emotional Anatomy: The Structure of Experience* 90). The confessor is not an inanimate listening device but another human being, subject to the same fears and emotions as those whose private disclosures he hears. He not only hears confession, but sees and senses it.

San Manuel Bueno, mártir undermines the very notion of beatification, and does so through confessional revelations; a traditional religious practice thus destabilizes a fundamental dogma. Blaming Ángela's hyper anxiety on extensive reading, don Manuel warns her with a statement that is fundamental to the entire novel: "¿Y dónde has leído eso, marisabidilla? Todo eso es literatura. No te des demasiado a ella, ni siquiera a Santa Teresa" (*SMBM* 112). By cautioning his penitent (through the authorized confessional ritual) against what historically has been regarded as a foundational Catholic confessional work, the priest questions the validity of beatification, as well as the ecclesiastical hierarchy that controls the beatification process. Teresa is *Santa* Teresa, yet her writing cannot be fully trusted. Likewise, as we learn from Ángela's confession, *san* Manuel is not the saint he outwardly appears to be. Moreover, Ángela learns from her brother Lázaro that don Manuel "acabó confesándome que creía que más de uno de los más grandes santos, acaso el mayor, había muerto sin creer en la otra vida" (143). By reporting her brother's verbal confession within her own written confession about a doubting priest, Ángela casts doubt upon the true convictions of venerated saints of all ages, and upon the validity of beatification itself. She identifies her priest and his disciples with a timeless community of unbelievers, united in their concealed doubts about the truths they overtly profess.

In her first confession, Ángela assumes the role of unauthorized priestess as she suddenly becomes a confessor in her own right. As if playing a subtle interpretive game of divining the mental state of don Manuel, Ángela perceives something "como una callada confesión suya en el susurro sumiso de su voz" (112). Feeling a priest(ess)-like need to console her unusual penitent, she returns to don Manuel "a confesarme con él para consolarle" (112). Thereafter, her role as confessor continues until the cleric's demise. She learns that the priest is an ordained unbeliever who does not believe in Satan, heaven or hell (113-14). After learning that don Manuel does not subscribe to the traditional principles of the Church he represents, Ángela hesitatingly returns to the confessional, but they feel uncomfortable and communicate in silence as both shed tears. Initially, he plays the confessor role and receives an affirmative answer when he asks if she believes. She then reverses the confessional roles and asks him pointedly: "Pero usted, padre, ¿cree usted?" (125). When Ángela grills him about his faith in the hereafter, the penitent saintly unbeliever sobbingly begs, "¡Mira, hija, dejemos eso!" (125-26). He then confesses his belief in the importance of life: "Hay que vivir. Y hay que dar vida" (126). He acknowledges her as his confessor, and then asks for absolution, which she grants: "En nombre de Dios Padre, Hijo y Espíritu Santo, le absuelvo, padre" (127).

Lázaro, who also emerges as a confessor to the priest, participates in an unusual multilevel, multigenerational confessional web. Don Manuel's deceased biological father, who had been plagued by an inclination toward suicide, confesses his problem to his son who, in turn, confesses his own inherited suicidal proclivity to his confessor Lázaro. Neither father nor son acts on the destructive impulses that haunt them, but this struggle against self-destruction reverberates throughout the son's persistent pleas to help people face life: "que vivan ellos" (*SMBM* 128). In this sequence of confessions, Don Manuel acts as both confessor and penitent, hearing the confession of his father and making his own secret admission (into which his father's confession is embedded) to Lázaro. Ultimately, the confessional chain includes a number of interrelated confessions: the priest's father confesses to don Manuel, who confesses to Lázaro, who confesses to Ángela, who writes a confession that reflects Unamuno's own personal confession.

As a confessant, the priest doubts that divine mediation brings absolution that extends to a post-mortal realm. His confession is one of action and service, a relentless confessional drama. His obsession with constant activity leads him to eschew quiet time alone. He never writes his own confession—that lot falls to Ángela Carballino—and in fact leaves virtually nothing of his own writing. Teaching, helping, entertaining, assisting, and comforting are his confession. An unusual martyr, Don Manuel surrenders his life by consecrating it to his community, which applauds his performative confession without understanding it (*SMBM* 104-09). He opts to confess through public performance: "Mi monasterio es Valverde de Lucerna" (109).

When confessing the truth to his sister about the priest's lack of faith, Lázaro mimics his master's emotions and becomes "tan pálido y tan tembloroso como don Manuel cuando le dio la comunión" (*SMBM* 121). What ensues is a confessional scene in which the unauthorized deaconess, like a spiritual mother to her confessing sibling, hears two confessions: those of her brother and of Don Manuel (120-23). This performative ceremony occurs outside the orthodox confessional setting and is conducted by an unlawful female priestess (Mario A. Ortiz, "*San Manuel bueno, mártir*: Divina novela de Miguel de Unamuno, archimensajero" 733). As Root argues, confession cannot be "confined to the ear of the priest or the door of the church" (13). Lázaro, "como en íntima confesión doméstica y familiar" (*SMBM* 121), discloses how don Manuel, in an outdoor setting, had urged him to uphold public unity by pretending to conform to the religious practices of the community (121-2). The priest assures him that he will not impose mainstream religion upon him, nor outwardly pressure him to experience inward religious conversion. When Lázaro, acting the part of a priest, probes to determine if don Manuel has strengthened his faith by officiating in the Mass, "él bajo la mirada al lago y se le llenaron los ojos de lágrimas" (122). Thus, by observing the priests' words, silence, gestures and emotion, Lázaro learns the secret that he now reveals to Ángela (121-2). The cleric's confession is encompassed by that of Lázaro, and both private admissions are embedded in the secret written confession of Ángela Carballino that comprises the novel.

On another occasion in which Lázaro acts the part of an unordained priest, he questions don Manuel about "la verdad, la verdad ante todo" (122). The priestly penitent's rhetorical style then reveals at least as much as the content of his confession. Trembling, he whispers in his confessor's ear, although they are alone in a rural setting. Don Manuel confesses his belief that common people are incapable of coping with a truth that is as terrible and intolerable as that which he knows. He discloses several heretical beliefs: that immortality is but a dream that humans dream, that there is not a single true church, and that consoling people is his goal, even if he must avoid the truth to do so (123-4).

Although Lázaro is don Manuel's key subordinate, his sister Ángela is both don Manuel's disciple and confessional chronicler. Because the bishop has initiated beatification proceedings for Don Manuel, she pens her confession, which she knows is more complete than that of the investigating prelate; "quiero dejar aquí consignado, a modo de confesión y sólo Dios sabe, que no yo, con qué destino, todo lo que sé y recuerdo de aquel varón matriarcal que llenó toda la más entrañada vida de mi alma, que fue mi verdadero padre espiritual, el padre de mi espíritu, del mío, el de Ángela Carballino" (*SMBM* 95-6). Ángela reflects his anti-monastical view when she refers to Valverde de Lucerna as "nuestro monasterio" (111). When her mother warns her to stop confessing so much or she will end up being a nun, Ángela rejects the idea and equates her village with a convent (113). Her position as a female cleric is unorthodox and lies beyond that accepted by the official Church. She regards don Manuel as a spiritual father and she reciprocates by serving him as a spiritual mother.

Part of don Manuel's confession is acted out by Blasillo, the town fool, who serves as a supporting witness to his views. After the priest recites the anguished cry, "¡Dios mío, Dios mío!, ¿por qué me has abandonado?" (*SMBM* 101-02), Blasillo soon repeats the statement verbatim. His perlocutionary power, like that of the priest he mimics, moves the congregation to tears (102). Following a confessional conversation with Ángela, in which the priest conveys his doubt in the devil's reality, she encounters Blasillo, who renews his imitation, "My God, my God, why hast Thou forsaken me?" (113). Ángela is so moved by Blasillo's angst-filled impersonation that she secludes herself in her room to weep. Her mother misinterprets this emotional reaction, which she believes is the result of excessive confession to the don Manuel (113).

Blasillo's impassioned cries echo don Manuel's heartfelt confession. Their words are the same, the rhetorical power of their voices is similar, and their perlocutionary effect on others is comparable. As don Manuel's nears death, his spirit wanes, his voice weakens, and tears flow for no perceptible reason. Blasillo mirrors his saintly counterpart's emotions and also weeps easily as he nears his own death. During his "última Semana de Pasión," don Manuel utters, for the last time, "¡Dios mío, Dios mío!, ¿por qué me has abandonado?" (134). On this occasion, as he gives communion to Lázaro, he neither wavers nor drops the wafer. He whispers a confession to his disciple, and unauthorized male confessor: "No hay más vida eterna que ésta . . ., que la sueñen eterna" (134). He urges his unauthorized female confessor, Ángela Carballino, "¡Reza, hija mía, reza!" (134). San Manuel dies while holding the hand of Blasillo, who also expires: "Así que hubo que enterrar dos cuerpos" (140). The priest passes away as the community recites that part of the *Credo* he has rejected: "resurrección de la carne y la vida perdurable" (140). The parallel course of the two lives—their sorrowful outbursts, their displays of emotion, their simultaneous deaths—suggests the possibility that the priest is one of don Manuel's disciples, an associate in the Holy Mother Church of Valverde de Lucerna, and a saintly double whose performative confession, like that of the priest, is written by Ángela Carballino.

The final disciple of san Manuel seems to be Unamuno himself, in his fictional form as a character in the novel, and as the novel's living author. In his epilogue to *San Manuel Bueno, mártir*, Unamuno insists that he must not reveal how Ángela Carballino's document has come into his hands. The fact that ecclesiastical authorities are not allowed access to her confession implies that only authorized individuals are privy to it. Since the fictional Unamuno mysteriously has it in his possession, we may assume that he has been given access to it because he is authorized due to his sympathy for the views enunciated in her written confession.[5] Thus, Unamuno seems to be a disciple of that other church led by san Manuel, that institution of good works, theological doubts, male and female clerics, skeptical intellectuals, and benevolent fools. Douglas M. Carey and Phillip G. Williams suggest that "the novel comprises a kind of fictional autobiography of the author himself, the chronicle of one man's anguished struggle to believe" (308); both character and author "struggle between faith and doubt" ("Religious Confession as Perspective and Mediation in Unamuno's *San Manuel Bueno, mártir*."309). *Character* Unamuno has faith in the unbelieving saint of Valverde de Lucerna, and trusts the *word* of his spiritual disciple and chronicler: "De la realidad de este san Manuel Bueno, mártir, tal como me lo ha revelado su discípula e hija espiritual Ángela Carballino, de esta realidad no se me ocurre dudar" (*SMBM* 148). *Author* Unamuno uses the confessional form to provide an intimate communication, and to construct an aura of credibility so that he may more effectively lash out at the prevailing rigidity of Catholic dogma through a fictional priest whose ambivalent confession parallels his own: "Jamás en sus sermones se ponía a declarar contra impíos, masones, liberales o herejes" (104).

In *San Manuel Bueno, mártir*, Unamuno achieves a metaconfessional narrative; with confessional episodes embedded within a work that itself has a confessional framework. His text secularizes religious confession by permitting an unordained female and her unordained brother to usurp sacerdotal prerogative. The author also blurs the line between confessor and confessant, particularly as Ángela and don Manuel interchange roles in confessional scenes. Unamuno demonstrates the performative nature of confession, and places greater value on confessional *works* than on penitential *words*; "las palabras no sirven para apoyar las obras, sino que las obras se bastan. Y para un pueblo como el de Valverde de Lucerna no hay más confesión que la conducta" (149).

San Manuel Bueno, mártir portrays don Manuel's performative pilgrimage, a saint's life that doubles as his confession. His confession is an unorthodox and deconstructive act that replaces *faith-good works* with *unbelief-good works*. Cause and effect seem to be detached from their traditional moorings. Bakhtin's theory of heteroglossia, with its emphasis on non-linguistic influences, helps us unravel the meaning of confession as Unamuno applies it to a small religious community and to Catholic Spain generally. Much of the background meaning in Ángela's culturally-infused confession is non-linguistic. Only with this background in mind can we start to comprehend the deep meaning behind don Manuel's creation of an alternative church, one that does not force intellectual conformity, doctrinal rigidity, or blind faith in an established *Credo*.

Unamuno's text addresses the interaction between community and confession. It acknowledges the social-emotional-psychological benefits of confession while undermining the miraculous. It replies to crucial existential questions with disquieting answers that are revealed privately through confessional interactions. Unamuno's text employs confession as a vehicle by which to question the very foundations of sainthood, Catholicism, and human life itself. It portrays confession as a rhetorical activity aimed at persuading others and comprehending oneself, a complex speech act that features words, gestures, and emotions. It is an intensely human, and humane, practice that shrinks the power and authority of clerics, and expands the boundaries of the confessional.

The Impious Confessor: Sender's Réquiem por un campesino español

A different variation on the theme of the unbelieving priest is found in Ramón Sender's *Réquiem por un campesino español* (1950),[6] a novel that recounts the tragic death of the peasant Paco el del Molino during the Spanish Civil War. A far cry from the protagonist in *San Manuel Bueno, mártir*, the confession of Mosén Millán, the local priest who figures prominently in Paco's life and death, exposes a priest whose collusion with fascists endangers his parishioners. The cleric's confession is revealed by the anonymous narrator of the novel. Sender's work, along with others in this chapter, demonstrates how confessional literature need not be restricted to first person narratives. Sender's *Réquiem* is a third person confession of the culpability of four men who are the most responsible for Paco's death. Although the peasant is well liked by his community (10), the treachery of powerful individuals—don Valeriano, don Gumersindo, Cástulo Pérez, and Mosén Millán—eventually costs him his life. Don Valeriano, a rich landowner and mayor who works under a wealthy proprietor and *duque*,[7] is a particularly dangerous enemy (10, 44-5). With the help of violent *señoritos*, young well-to-do thugs, he becomes mayor of an unnamed location, which suggests that local terror and casualties are but part of a larger pattern of abusive fascist activity. A second enemy who harasses Paco is don Gumersindo, who cynically boasts of his merciful and kind nature (10, 23, 47, 65-66). A third adversary is Cástulo Pérez, a slippery and enigmatic man who feigns friendship with Paco, a treacherous foe who represents the difficulty of knowing where to place one's trust during the Civil War years (10, 23). Finally, Mosén Millán is a spineless priest who performs his ecclesiastical duties in a way that shields himself from danger, and ingratiates himself with the social elite. He is willing to break confidences and endanger others in order to protect himself.

Mosén Millán is sympathetic to Paco el del Molino and is willing to serve him as long as such service is not personally threatening. The wedding ceremony he performs for Paco and his bride Águeda becomes a symbol of impending death, rather than newness of life, for the couple and their offspring. Having administered baptism, confirmation, and first communion to the groom in earlier years, Mosén Millán chats with the couple at the marriage service. He makes reference to past, present, and future beds that he has blessed, is blessing, or will bless as a cleric. The first is that of Paco the infant, the second of Paco the husband, and the third (which seems irrelevant at the time) of Paco the dead man (54). Cástulo Pérez unexpectedly arrives in his car for the wedding and assists Paco and Águeda with transportation. This automobile later plays a significant role in the confessional scene associated with Paco's death.

The shoemaker, a nameless character in Sender's novel, is present at the wedding, dressed in his own wedding suit (56). Just as his marriage precedes that of Paco, so does his death (82). Ultimately, both fall victim to fascist cruelty during the Civil War. The shoemaker is regarded as an enemy to the powerful political and religious interests represented by the *duque*, don Valeriano, don Gumersindo, Cástulo Pérez, and Mosén Millán. By the time of the shoemaker's death, Paco has gone into hiding for his own safety (82). The link between matrimony and death (a potent symbol of dashed hopes and extinguished life) is strengthened when Paco, his wife now pregnant, is executed (101-03). In a display of extraordinary religious hypocrisy, Paco's executioners delay this political assassination until their prey has confessed to Mosén Millán. On an earlier occasion, the cleric had complained to Mayor Cástulo Pérez that his henchmen had not allowed six assassinated peasants to confess prior to their executions (81). Confession thus becomes a heartless ritual, a pious accomplice to impious brutality.

The final confession of Paco el del Molino is enacted in a makeshift confessional, Cástulo Pérez's automobile. The same vehicle that had transported Paco and his bride on their wedding day now conveys Paco toward the deadly third bed of which Mosén Millán had prophesied at the nuptial ceremony (65, 99). The car's running board provides an uncomfortable space for the penitent to kneel while the car seat within presents the confessor with a comfortable place to practice his duplicitous craft. An open door facilitates confessional conversation and temporarily prolongs Paco's life (99). This confessional car, a symbol of economic-political-religious collusion, mocks the religious sacrament. The improvised confessional, like Cástulo's vehicle itself, denotes power, movement, domination, and hegemony. Penitents become part of a hegemonic machine as confessions are reduced to empty spiritual rituals shrouded in secular intrigue and coercion.

The priest's young *monaguillo* (assistant or altar boy), recites a *romance* (popular ballad) that frames *Réquiem,* a novelistic confession that reveals the complicity of church and state in wronging Paco and others. Two parallel confessions recount the tale of guilt and assassination: the textual narrative and the *romance*. The *romance* (18), etched in the unnamed altar boy's memory, is a popular ballad, and he knows only some of the verses (11). The ballad identifies Mosén Millán as one who baptizes Paco and later hears his confession from the automobile-confessional (65). The *romance* mirrors reality but also contains flawed perceptions. It relates how the priest receives Paco's confession of sins (65), a term that taints the character of the cleric more than that of his upright victim. It claims that Paco weeps (11), but the *monaguillo*—in Cástulo Pérez's car assisting the priest—denies that Paco's weeping is about the threat to his life (11). This lack of tears at the final confession, coupled with Paco's failure to understand the priest's repeated references to sins, highlights the contrived character of the confession. Only after being asked a fourth time is his repentance has been complete (101) does Paco consent, not with words but through a gesture, the nodding of his head (101). As with two previous victims who perish in the confession-execution ritual, the priest's declaration of absolution (99-102)—signals Paco's imminent murder. The cleric's verbalization of the words of pardon (102) is accompanied by a raising of the hand (102). This combination of gesture and speech functions as an indirect speech act in which the granting of spiritual life doubles as the sign of physical death. Like the bifurcated individual he is, Mosén Millán serves as supporter and spy, friend and foe, healer and henchman.

Hypocrisy blends with irony as absolution invites death. Paco does not succumb immediately after the first shots are fired, although the other two men instantly fall to the ground. He runs toward a sanctuary where he hopes to find refuge: the car-confessional. The door that serves as a conduit for the confession of imaginary sins is now shut; an open door is no longer part of the brutal ritual. The priest who acknowledges the innocence of the three condemned men, while claiming to be powerless to help (100), now refuses to open the car door, the portal to the confessional and to extended life. Paco's blood stains the car (102). Despite his pleas for priestly mediation to save his life, the impious holy man refuses. His eyes closed, as if to feign ignorance and deny responsibility, he prays (102). Someone protests as Paco is about to be shot next to the place of confession, so he is taken to the nearby wall where the others had been executed, the wall from which he had fled. Shots ring out and the betrayed victim dies muttering accusing words that are heard by the traitorous priest (103).

Paco, who has sympathized with the impoverished and powerless of his nation, now finds himself defenseless. When the priest abruptly denies Paco access to the confessional, he exemplifies the fascist penchant for ignoring the cries of the oppressed, including Jews (33) and impoverished Spaniards living in caves (61). The ritual of confession and death is no coincidental overlap of secular and political activity; it is an intentional commission of dark deeds illuminated by the lights of Cástulo Pérez's vehicle. The headlights are illuminated as the first bullets are fired, then extinguished after all three innocent men have been killed (102-3). The lights themselves become part of the dark ritual.

Mosén Millán uses the authority, prestige and trust that are invested in his priestly office to bring Paco out of hiding. First, he employs a deceptive stratagem to learn Paco's whereabouts from Paco's father. Too ethically weak to keep this confidential information a secret, he reveals Paco's location to his enemies (87-89). Although he assures Paco that he will not be harmed, the priest proves more eager to please his powerful associates—don Valeriano, don Gumersindo, and Cástulo Pérez—than to risk his own safety for those he knows are innocent. Even as he exerts religious hegemony over Paco and others who confess to him as a priest, Mosén Millán submits to the hegemonic power of the growing fascist regime by personally enticing Paco, on false pretenses, to come out of hiding.

A year after Paco's execution, a gathering of the guilty occurs, and a symbolic reenactment of the atrocity takes place in the temple itself. The *monaguillo* sees a colt that has inexplicably entered the church; the doors have been shut. The three guilty men—don Valeriano, don Gumersindo, and Cástulo Pérez—see more clearly and reveal that the animal is the riderless colt of Paco el del Molino. It happily and freely prances about, frustrating the expulsion efforts of the three men, who act in response to Mosén Millán's request to remove the animal. Finally, after light enters the sanctuary, the colt decides that the church is the church is not a place where he is welcome (95). The colt, like his deceased owner, is driven from the church which previously had been a place of contentment (92-5). After the colt exits the temple, the doors, like the car-confessional doors a year earlier, are shut and darkness prevails (95, 103). There is light while Paco lives and while his colt moves freely about the church building; after each is persecuted by Paco's enemies, darkness replaces light.

In Sender's novel, the innocent confess while the guilty persecute. The confessor sits *inside* his vehicle of power, while innocent penitents kneel *outside*. Light illuminates dark deeds; closed priestly eyes recall ghastly events. A *romance* reveals the tragedy of Paco's death; an innocent *monaguillo* confesses the deeds of his religious superior and the powerful fascists with whom he is allied. The novel validates Bakhtin's theory of heteroglossia; non-linguistic factors, including the political climate in Spain as fascists assert hegemony over the Church, are crucial to the fictional plot, and the historical reality of Civil War. Mosén Millán's confessional becomes a panopticon that jeopardizes life rather than a place of healing where confidences can be safely divulged.

As we have seen in this and in other literary works, confessional writing is commonly autobiographical but it is a mistake to assume that such is always the case. Confessional literature is an independent genre that may combine with any other without being subservient to it. It is a genre of crisis that is modeled, in either its sacred or secular varieties, after the religious sacrament of penitence. Crisis and the quest for liberation characterize each of the works we have discussed. "La historia del cautivo" from *Don Quijote*, is autobiographical, but the novel in general is not. Gutiérrez's novel *Cornelia Bororquia* utilizes the epistolary genre, which features first-person writing, but the authors of the letters that comprise the novel describe confessional scenes involving external actors. Unamuno's *San Manuel Bueno, mártir* is a first-person confession but it is *primarily* a third-person confession *about* an unbelieving priest. Even within clearly autobiographical confessional writings, there are many embedded scenes that are not autobiographical. An awareness of the existence of confessional frames and interjected confessional scenes enriches our reading of works of Spanish literature. Substantially greater insights regarding confession result when we pay greater attention to confessional scenes that feature non-protagonists, and when the possibilities of group, even national, confession are explored.

Chapter Five

"Es de Lope": The Drama of Confession and *Fuente Ovejuna*[1]

Lope de Vega transformed Spanish drama from an often cumbersome style, characterized by long speeches and slow action, to a more engaging form that facilitated the creation of a national theater.[2] His *Fuente Ovejuna* plays a role in the flourishing of this national theater (Francisco Ruiz Ramón, *Historia del teatro español, desde sus orígenes hasta 1900* 104, 127, 148-49; Hesse 9). He played the leading role in establishing the "national history play," and in so doing not only delved into Spain's historical past but also its religious (including confession) and institutional (including the Inquisition) heritage (Walter Cohen, *Drama of a Nation: Public Theater in Renaissance England and Spain* 253). His standard three-act technique presented a central problem in the first act, elaborated on the problem's complications in Act 2, and then provided a resolution in the final act (Lope, *Arte nuevo de hacer comedias en este tiempo*). In *Fuente Ovejuna* (1612-1614),[3] the third-act denouement utilizes confession as a vehicle to demonstrate the superiority of benevolent monarchy to local tyranny. Two modes of confession seek to break the impasse of how to punish a whole village while seeking to gain their loyalty to the monarch. The first mode, a series of violent inquisitorial confessions supervised by a vengeful judge, fails to provide resolution.[4] The second, a pastoral mode utilized by the Catholic Monarch Fernando, who performs as a great secular archbishop, succeeds in resolving the drama's plot and offering a national solution to regional despotism.

The grand confessional scene with which the drama closes privileges the benevolent imposition of a merciful justice over the harsh inquisitorial confessional practices that provide only unforgiving injustice. Lope's skillful blending of pastoral confession and monarchical supremacy is a dual attack that at once proclaims the superiority of orderly centralized rule over chaotic regional politics, and the desirable ascendancy of just confessional practices over the cruel inquisitorial counterpart that was becoming increasingly entrenched in Spanish life. This fusion of pastoral confession and monarchical rule utilizes pastoral confession to redeem both individuals and the emerging Spanish nation. As with confession generally, it emerges out of inner tension and perceived personal peril. Confession rescues Fuente Ovejuna, and it redeems Spain.[5]

Confessional literature, including theatrical works, is *seen* as well as *heard*; it includes gestures as well as speech. Because of their intrinsic emphasis on performance, theatrical texts afford exceptionally clear examples of the nonverbal (kinesthetic) aspects of confession. Dramatic works are written specifically for the stage and commonly include stage directions that call for gestures, emotions, and movements. Even without such instructions, each confessional scene is performative because confession is an intrinsically kinesthetic activity. Playwrights compose their dramas with an eye toward enactment on a theatrical stage, and their confessional scenes are particularly compelling because they spring from human dilemmas and evoke human emotions. The element of secrecy associated with confession—whether pastoral, inquisitorial, or juridical—entices readers and viewers to uncover confidential information, to *see* the unknown.

Surprisingly, while critics have written much about *Fuente Ovejuna*—Lope de Vega's classic written "con bárbara y sublime poesía" (Sanchez-Cortés 5)—they have not yet tapped its bursting confessional possibilities that culminate in a spectacular group confession. *Fuente Ovejuna* is an artistic version of an alleged April 1476 occurrence in which the entire village of Fuente Ovejuna acts with solidarity to oppose a local tyrant, Fernán Gómez de Guzmán. By the time Lope pens his drama, the event already has become part of popular folklore (Alberto Castilla, "Conflictos sociales" 86). By the early seventeenth century, confession (religious, inquisitorial, and juridical) is so deeply entrenched in Spanish religious and secular life that its inclusion in this play provides a unifying theme that buttresses Lope's encouragement of a national theater. Although what actually occurs historically has been disputed, Lope's theatrical version immortalizes the event and the historical mythology surrounding the event (Hall 11-19).[6] This play demonstrates Terrence Doody's contention that every confession has links to a larger community (7, 185). While this is true of the play's minor individual confessional scenes, it is particularly evident in the dramatic group confession. National themes, national religion, and national monarchs each reinforce a truly national theater.

The Fourth Lateran Council (1215) required all Catholics to confess, in private, to a priest at least annually. Routine access to true privacy, however, continued to be problematic even in the period during and after the mid sixteenth-century Council of Trent. In spite of breaches in confidentiality, the ideal of the private confession was clearly established in the 1215 Council. In the four centuries prior to this historic gathering, emphasis on personal contrition had increased, even as penitential penalties had decreased. The mediatory role of the priest had received greater stress during this period, as had the relationship between private confession and spiritual healing at the hands of a "skilled doctor," the priest (Tentler, *Sin and Confession* 16).[7]

Lope's dramatic recreation of the presumed, but likely mythical, 1476 group confession at Tordesillas finds its parallel in the age old religious ritual, but it also departs from that tradition. By the reign of Fernando and Isabel, two and a half centuries had elapsed since the Fourth Lateran Council (1215) had encouraged annual private confession to one's own priest. In Lope's drama, the *Catholic* Monarchs assume a priest-like role as they hear a *public* and *collective* confession that includes a statement of loyalty to the Catholic *Monarchs*.[8] These secular sovereigns, objects of seventeenth century veneration (Victor Dixon, "'Su majestad habla, en fin, como quien tanto ha acertado': La conclusión ejemplar de Fuente Ovejuna" 165), are depicted as veritable healers of the realm who act in the spirit of the instructions given to priests by the Fourth Lateran Council: "Let him carefully inquire about the circumstances of both the sinner and the sin, so that he may prudently discern what sort of advice he ought to give and what remedy to apply, using various means to heal the sick person" ("Fourth Lateran Council—1215 A.D."). In the final confessional scene, Fernando plays the leading role as confessor, consistent with "the role of patriarchy as a dominant ideology in early modern society and theatre" (Ivan Cañadas, "Class, Gender and Community in Thomas Dekker's *The Shoemaker's Holiday* and Lope de Vega's *Fuente Ovejuna*" 137). His confessional role, like Lope's drama in general, demonstrates that confession is "not simply . . . a sacramental act, but . . . a historically grounded . . . means of shaping the individual and the society" (Lualdi and Thayer, "Introduction," *Penitence* 1).

In 1551-1552, the Fourteenth Session of the Council of Trent (1545-1563) reiterated and clarified the Catholic Church's position on the sacrament of penance, including the need for confession, as it did on so many issues during this historic response to the turmoil unleashed by Luther's posting of ninety-five critical theses at a Wittenberg church in 1517. Confession was a major issue in both the Protestant Reformation and the Catholic Counter-Reformation, and major theologians (Luther, Eck, Calvin) and orders (Jesuits, Barnabites, Theatines) sought to interpret its proper religious and social roles (de Boer, "The Politics of the Soul: Confession in Counter-Reformation Milan" 118). The Jesuits, for example, maintained that "confession was a crucial step towards union with God" and personal consolation (Michael Maher, "Confession and consolation: the Society of Jesus and Its Promotion of the General Confession" 185, 200), and used theatrical means to urge confession (Jennifer D. Selwyn, "'Schools of Mortification': Theatricality and the Role of Penitential Practice in the Jesuits' Popular Missions" 202-03, 212-13). The Jesuit luminary Ignatius Loyola and his disciple Pedro de Ribadeneyra pressed for a "renewed, activist Catholicism" (Bilinkoff, "The Many 'Lives' of Pedro de Ribadeneyra" 181). The council of Trent, which represented an important historical milestone for the audiences that first viewed Lope's *Fuente Ovejuna*, was still over four decades in the future for the 1476 villagers of Fuente Ovejuna who opposed their tyrannical *Comendador*.[9] Lope's interweaving of past and present, priest and monarch, Church and state, skillfully reinforces the doctrinal pronouncements of the Fourth Lateran

Council and the Council of Trent, reaffirms the unifying power of monarchy, and underscores the importance of both words in the title *Catholic Monarchs*.

Although the confessional ritual changed over time, individuals were expected to confess individually. Beginning in the sixth century, greater emphasis was placed on confessional privacy than had previously been the case. As a result of the Council of Trent, yet greater privacy became the norm. This privacy, however, was more *verbal* than *visual*. Adequate space between waiting confessants generally provided *verbal* privacy, even before the introduction of the private confessional booth in the sixteenth century, and its widespread use in the seventeenth (Anthony Low, "Privacy, Community, and Society: Confession as a Cultural Indicator in *Sir Gawain and the Green Knight*" 4-5).[10] *Performative* privacy, however, was not stressed prior to the use of the booths. In the pre-Tridentine period in particular, emotions and gestures were open to public gaze. This rendered *private* confession a substantially *public* endeavor. Lope's group confessional scene, which does not appear in Fray Francisco de Rades y Andrada's historical account (*Crónica de la Orden de Calatrava*), obviously breaks from the pastoral norm for *either* the era of the Fuente Ovejuna incident (1476) or that of its dramatic Lopean depiction (1612-1614). Lope grants the collective protagonist neither *verbal* nor *visual* privacy, yet he appears to have appropriated and adapted the religious ritual to blend the villager's *confession* and plea for clemency with their *profession* of loyalty to the emerging nation-state. He also dramatically portrays how confession is *both* an individual quest for liberation from intense personal crisis *and* a restorative ritual that binds the errant penitent to the larger community.

Even this profession of loyalty takes on a confessional aspect. In Lope's highly allegorical work, the united penitence of an entire town may be viewed as the confession of an emerging Spanish nation, a collective penitent following a "conversion model, which represents the hero moving from sin to holiness" (Rhodes 94). The confessant-village commits to abandon *political sin* (of maintaining regional loyalties) and to embrace the increasingly centralized rule of their *holinesses*, the Catholic Monarchs. Fuente Ovejuna had been the victim the immoral and ruthless *Comendador* Fernán Gómez de Guzmán, of the military Order of Calatrava.[11] In 1464, twelve years before Fuente Ovejuna overthrew the *Comendador*, Isabel had successfully weakened the Order of Santiago. Beginning in 1475, Fernando and Isabel agreed that public insurrections that furthered crown interests were acceptable and would not be punished. Lope uses confession to dramatize this royal position. The historical rebellion by Fuente Ovejuna, around which Lope crafts his drama, occurred the following year, 1476 (Hesse 12). The Comendador not only posed a threat to feminine virtue but also to the rule of the Catholic Monarchs because of his loyalty to Alfonso V of Portugal, a bitter rival of Fernando and Isabel, who actively sought to dethrone them (F. García Pavón 14-15; Castilla, "Conflictos sociales" 85). Although the Order is allegedly comprised of exemplary knights who are refined by "vows of poverty, obedience and conjugal chastity" (*Brewer*, "Calatrava, Order of"), Lope represents the aging institution as a corrupt association that covets special privilege, opposes national authority, engenders disorder, and mocks moral virtue. Gómez, the Order's tyrannical leader who controls the *encomienda* of Fuente Ovejuna as one of the "jurisdicciones privilegiadas" (Marcelino Menéndez y Pelayo, *Antología General de Menéndez Pelayo: Recopilación orgánica de su doctrina* II: 719), personifies evil while the Catholic Monarchs epitomize good (Dixon 165).

Fernán Gómez's threat to Fuente Ovejuna typifies the nobility's threat to the integrity of the *aldea*, that rural repository of paradisiacal goodness, of pastoral simplicity, of curative environment (Constance Rose, "Corte y aldea" 92; G. W. Ribbans, "Significado y estructura de 'Fuenteovejuna'" 92-94). The citizens of Fuente Ovejuna, that "idyllic island of Primitivism in which the values of the Golden Age are still miraculously preserved" (Leo Spitzer, "A Central Theme and its Structural Equivalent in Lope's 'Fuenteovejuna'" 400n), become enraged at the *Comendador*'s abusive behavior and discuss alternatives. Some believe that the town itself is in jeopardy. Concerned that the entire village's reputation (*honra*) is in jeopardy, Esteban asks, "Respondedme: ¿hay alguno de vosotros / que no esté lastimado en honra y vida?"(1669-70).[12] The group is surprised at the sudden entrance of Laurencia, who is furious at her father "porque dejas que me roben / tiranos sin que me vengues, / traidores sin que me cobres" (1725-27). She labels the men "sheep" and bitterly censures, "Ovejas sois, bien lo dice / de Fuente Ovejuna el nombre" (1758-59). The men later prove that they are neither cowardly nor infidels when they slay the *Comendador*, refuse to confess to the deed, and confess their loyalty to the Catholic Monarchs.

Acting in the belligerent *mujer varonil* tradition (Hall 25), Laurencia then organizes the women of the town, and urges a return of "aquel siglo de amazonas" (1792). Stirred by Laurencia's impassioned speech—"Liebres cobardes nacistes; / bárbaros sois, no españoles" (1768-69)—the men determine to join the women in a fight against the *Comendador*, rallied by the cry of "¡Traidores tiranos mueran!" (1814). The villagers, now a collective protagonist (a communal *villano digno*; Juan Manuel Escudero Baztán, "Villanos" 317-18), seek to avenge the wrongs committed by the *Comendador* and, while he is directing the punishment of Frondoso, they approach the Calatravan's house. His subordinate Flores exclaims, "¡El pueblo junto viene!" (1857), while Fernán Gómez anxiously views the ominous public unity in personal terms: "¿El pueblo, contra mí?" (1860). Frightened, the *Comendador* has Frondoso untied and urges him to calm the mayor (1862-63). Frondoso refuses to cooperate with the town's oppressor and casts his lot with the enraged peasants. Gómez, suddenly a tyrant turned *penitent*, desperately looks to the people of Fuente Ovejuna for mercy. The plural protagonist becomes a collective *confessor* as their abusive penitent begs, "¡Pueblo esperad!" (1879). But the people are in no mood to grant either mercy or absolution: "¡Agravios nunca esperan!" (1879). Rejecting Gómez's claim, "¡Yo soy vuestro señor!" (1885), his unswayed confessors refuse to recognize any future homage due except to the Catholic lords: "¡Nuestros señores son los Reyes Católicos!" (1885-86).

The Fuente Ovejuna revolt is not born of revenge alone but is a means of restoring order under national leadership. The *Comendador* has jeopardized the Spanish throne through his treasonous alliance with the Portuguese monarch (McKendrick 89). The challenge to the social order is also represented in *Fuente Ovejuna* as a result of the challenge to societal honor. When the selfish appetites of the *Comendador* threaten communal harmony, the whole town responds and restores unity by eliminating the tyrant (Richard Young, *La figura del rey y la institución real en la comedia lopesca* 42n, 45n). The *sins* of Fernán Gómez are not only moral but also political. The town perceives his plea for mercy as simply a ploy to save his life rather than a transformational, and therefore genuine, confession. They grant no absolution to this composite Lucifer, Heliogabalus, and Nero.[13] The increasingly contrite *Comendador*, finding no pardon from the vassals who now control his destiny, shifts his emotional pleas to a divine interlocutor: "Ya muero. / ¡Piedad, Señor, que en tu clemencia espero" (1894-95). With these words, both his frantic plea for compassion and his life come to an end.[14] Last minute confession is of no avail to the *Comendador*. Confession, a liberty-seeking ritual, falls short of its perlocutionary objective. Confessants, whether in religious or secular spheres, typically confess to gain freedom from suffering, guilt, or other undesirable circumstances; confessors, through religious or secular power, choose how much healing balm to offer. Neither an earthly nor a heavenly mediator intervenes on behalf of the tyrant, who laments his punishment but not his own wrongdoings. His confessional rhetoric proves inadequate as does his ability to exert hegemonic influence over his newly empowered subjects.

Robert Fiore explains that according to sixteenth and seventeenth century beliefs in natural law, divinely sanctioned punishment awaits tyrants who fail to honor their obligations to their subjects (Fiore, *Drama and Ethos: Natural-Law Ethics in Spanish Golden Age Theater* 14). Failing to act the part required by his noble status ("no 'es quien es'"), Fernán Gómez courts disaster (Dian Fox, "Nobles" 226). Because natural law is accessible to humans and taps into God's eternal law (including the practice of confession; Tentler, *Sin and Confession* 57) historical or dramatic conflict vis-à-vis natural law is infused with strong ethical and metaphysical meaning (Fiore, "Ley natural" 192). Such is the case when Fuente Ovejuna's collective punitive action effectively purges the office of *Comendador* from the previous hierarchical arrangement of God, Monarch, *Comendador,* mayor and people, in that order. As Melveena McKendrick argues, "The political burden of the play is that seigniorial feudalism has yielded now for good to the central authority of monarchy; historically, never again would the barons rise in revolt against the Spanish Crown" (89). The Golden Age penchant for issues of "law, expressed as issues of *power* politics" finds rich expression in *Fuente Ovejuna* (Henry W. Sullivan, "Law, Desire, and the Double Plot: Toward a Psychoanalytic Poetics of the *Comedia*" 224; italics in original), as the powerful tie between the Crown and Church established by the Catholic Monarchs further concentrates power in royal hands. In *Fuente Ovejuna*, popular rebellion was not portrayed as tearing down social order but strengthening it, reestablishing it (Lázaro Carreter, *Lope de Vega, introducción a su vida y obra* 198).

Mengo, the town buffoon (a *gracioso* in the *villano cómico* tradition; Escudero Baztán 317), acting as both secular confessor and unofficial judge, refuses to free the *Comendador's* former assistants (64). Here, as on other occasions, Mengo's comical antics provide relief in a drama that deals with serious issues (Hall 23).[15] As the ancient rhetorician Quintilian notes, "Now, though laughter may seem to be a trivial matter, aroused often by buffoons (*scurrae*), actors of farce, or indeed fools, it nevertheless possesses perhaps the most commanding and irresistible force of all [and] it often turns the scale in very important matters, as it frequently dispels hatred and anger" (3: 67, 69).

Having suffered under the *Comendador's* rule, Jacinta and Pascuala now taunt Flores (1913) An emotional Flores appeals, "¡Piedad, señoras!" (1915). Ortuño also faces the wrath of the women, as Laurencia exhorts them to perform a symbolic gesture of justified vengeance: "¡Entrad, teñid las armas vencedoras / en estos viles!" (1917-18). In more favorable confessional settings, *tears*, *pity*, and *blood* bring mercy, absolution, and newness of life. Here they bring none of these.

In the next scene, at the residence of the Catholic Kings at Toro (a place name suggesting strength), a seriously weakened Flores (1957-59) notifies the king, "De Fuente Ovejuna vengo, / donde, con pecho inclemente, / los vecinos de la villa / a su señor dieron muerte" (1960-63). Although his interview with the king seems to be simply a recounting of the evil deeds of others, it is really much more than a political report. When we consider the *performative* nature of his actions and speech, we see that his flight to the palace may appropriately be interpreted as a multi-dimensional confession that reveals not only the actions and thoughts of the wounded Flores but also those of Fuente Ovejuna and the Spanish people generally.

Flores' confession is part of a pilgrimage of personal transformation and healing. The *Comendador's* shady subordinate flees Fuente Ovejuna for the royal palace, and symbolically exchanges the discredited Order of Calatrava for allegiance to a beneficent monarchy. His pilgrimage is an exodus from bondage to freedom, a common theme in the religious confessional tradition (Shirley Joan Paolini, "Towards an Understanding of the Self: The Confessional Mode in Dante's *Commedia* and St. Augustine's *Confessions*" 156). His is not only a flight *from* the location where the Order of Calatrava is under attack and *from* personal loyalty to Portugal, Juana la Beltraneja, and Alfonso V, but also a flight *toward* the palace, which doubles as protective fortress and curative infirmary, and *toward* a personal commitment to the *Reconquista*, which the Catholic Monarchs personify (Castilla 86).[16] Flores' very appearance before the king is a performative gesture that implicitly acknowledges the monarch's supremacy and the declining clout of regional military strongmen. Lope does not allow him to die, like the *Comendador*, at the hands of angry peasants; he opts to have him survive to confess his misguided loyalty to Portugal and his political rebirth, a change of heart that allows him to genuinely support the emerging Spanish nation.

Balancing justice and mercy, the king acts the part of a royal confessor who is both national judge and doctor.[17] This scene not only underscores the two historic roles of the religious confessor,[18] but also the increasing hegemony of the crown, to which Flores, like the burgeoning Spanish nation, now gives fealty. Thomas Tentler's succinct assertion about ecclesiastical jurisdiction applies, in this instance, to political dominion: "Jurisdiction [is] defined in answer to the question, 'To whom is one obliged to confess?'" (*Sin and Confession* 61). Clearly unable to secure either mercy or healing from the peasants, Flores obtains a sympathetic royal ear and assistance for his wounded body when he turns to the Sovereigns (67). Flores' symbolic pilgrimage to Toro invites the audience to contemplate the issue of jurisdiction and helps set the stage for the dramatic confession of the townspeople at the end of the play. Flowers (Flores) that hope to take root and flourish in Spain must align themselves with the monarchy. Opponents who continue to resist die, while those who turn from their deviant political behavior and confess the king's supremacy receive absolution, healing and a place in the Spanish kingdom. When Fernando the healer orders aid for Flores, who has previously opposed the Crown (2026-27), he offers him new life in a superior order and emblematically holds out the same hope to other former enemies. The Catholic Monarchs are eager to forgive and heal those who confess loyalty to their hegemony. As Tentler suggests, penitential practice involves "co-operation, not just top-down commandments" ("Postscript" 248).

Flores urges the king to avenge the death of his deceased lord, but ironically his itemization of Fuente Ovejuna's transgressions serves to describe the town's heroic stance against treason and its confession of support for the crown. The king subsequently determines to dispatch a judge, accompanied by a captain for protection, to inquire into the turmoil "y castigue los culpados / para ejemplo de las gentes" (2020-21). Mayor Esteban, predicting that the sovereigns will send an investigator to assess the turmoil in his town, takes a democratic approach and urges his people to unite: "Concertaos todos a una / en lo que habéis de decir" (2089-90). When Frondoso asks the mayor what they should confess when confronted by a juridical confessor, Esteban counsels that they simply admit that the whole town slew killed the *Comendador*. Frondoso expresses the unanimous view when he exclaims, "¡Fuente Ovejuna lo ha hecho!" (2095).[19] Through their repeated confession—which doubles as a nonconfession—they blend collective guilt with individual innocence, group penitence with individual impenitence. They perform an indirect speech act comprised of both speech and silence; they offer a public statement of fact but no admission of private guilt.

Notified by a councilman that the judge has arrived, accompanied by a military captain, the emboldened mayor categorizes the questioner as the devil. Laurencia expresses her fear of "el furor con que procede / aqueste pesquisidor" (2185-86) and urges her adored Frondoso, "Procura guardar la vida. / Huye tu daño, no esperes" (2187-88). Hearing cries from an elderly man (who proves to be Laurencia's father Esteban), Frondoso presumes they are the result of torture and urges her to pay close attention. To his plea "Déjenme un poco," the judge responds, "Ya os dejo. / Decid, ¿quién mató a Fernando?" (2206-07). Esteban, as uncooperative as he is impenitent, responds in the rehearsed manner. In a concurrent confessional scene, a boy is racked, but he too politely supplies the standard confession: "Fuente Ovejuna, señor" (2214). As Francisco Ruiz Ramón points out, Lope builds his torture scene around the courage of those considered least able to bear up under the Judge's violent confessional tactics: a boy, an old man, a town comic known for cowardliness, and a woman (*Historia del teatro español, desde sus orígenes hasta 1900* 159). Their mere presence carries symbolic importance.

By hearing what is done to others of their town, other peasants share in the terror of the occasion. These tormented cries of community members performing dramatic roles against their volition are heard by spectators (in the play itself) who are moved to compassion and outrage by scenes they would prefer not to witness. Torture adds a new rhetorical dimension to confession by transforming the confessional ritual from one of consolation to one of terror, and the confessor-penitent relationship from one of joint cooperation to one of mutual distrust. In this case, Lope's dramatic representation is based on historical reality, which presumably fortified its rhetorical effect on early audiences among whom "Fuente Ovejuna did it" had already become a commonplace expression.[20]

The judge is perplexed at the merriment of the townspeople—"Parece que los encantas" (2232)—and greets their repetitious confessions with orders to intensify the torture (2233) When Mengo is selected for interrogation, a listening Frondoso fears that he will confess (2239). After repeated cries of anguish, the town *gracioso* promises, "¡Ay, yo lo diré, señor!" (2244). After heightening the judge's expectations (2247-48), the comic resolutely repeats the stock confession, while applying an affectionate diminutive to the town's name: "Señor, Fuente Ovejunica" (2249). Annoyed and fatigued, the judge marvels that they mock the pain inflicted upon them and decides to leave the impenitent penitents to themselves (2251-54).

As Ivan Cañadas notes, "it is Mengo who breaks the judge's resolve" (148). Mengo's emotional and factual give-and-take with the judge provides an example of the interactive exchange of concepts in the confessional process. Besides the unforgettable "Fuente Ovejuna lo hizo," the concepts of group solidarity, defiance of tyranny, and collective courage stand out as practical consequences of this dramatic interchange. As speech act theorists Moulin and Rousseau maintain, people are more likely to remember the practical repercussions of an utterance than they are to recall a statement itself (184). One remembers and is moved more by Mengo's courage and the social issues he stands for than by his verbal utterances.

Lope's repetition of the confessional torture scene—rehearsal, performance and celebration—is an effective didactic technique that reinforces the ritualistic nature of confession. It also demonstrates how confessants seek liberty in situations other than pastoral settings, and how the confessor may either promote healing or inflict pain. Confession is an interactive process involving human choices, diverse motives, and unpredictable results. Lope's three-part approach involves significant repetition but also important differences with each iteration. The playwright's methodology involves a ritualistic unfolding that moves from apprehension to endurance to jubilation. By so doing, the confessional scenes suggest the challenges and joys associated with Spanish nation-building under the monarchs as well as the vastly different confessional outcomes that result from inquisitorial versus pastoral confessors.

Lope's play ends with confessions to the king by the Master of Calatrava, Rodrigo Téllez Girón, and then by the entire village of Fuente Ovejuna. The former has been an ally of Fernán Gómez, but expediently recognizes the need to mend his political ways and submit to the hegemonic control of the Catholic Monarchs. He now laments having succumbed to the evil and seditious plan of the *Comendador* to oppose the monarchy's unifying goal of providing "a peaceful and orderly existence" (Fiore, *Drama and Ethos* 16) for their subjects.[21] After being granted an audience with the Monarchs, Rodrigo assumes the role of penitent, and employs fitting language and gestures (75). He praises the monarchy, kneels, begs for pardon, and confesses to having been deceived: "Confieso que fui engañado" (2310-17, 2338). The kneeling Master of Calatrava pleads for forgiveness (2320-21), pledges his loyalty and (as if carrying out a penitential vow) promises to assist with "el valor que hay en mi espada" in the campaign against the Moors in Granada (2323-37). In a manner that parallels a common literary and religious motif, the monarch acts the part of a shepherd who rescues sheep that are threatened by wolves.[22]

When King Fernando, the healing confessor, commands Rodrigo, "Alzad, Maestre" (2338), the new convert to national supremacy gratefully acknowledges his pastoral sensitivity: "Sois de afligidos consuelo" (2341). Queen Isabel then commends the pilgrim's valor, which prompts him to wax eloquent in glowing praise for the sovereigns (2342-45). Rodrigo, now converted from political blindness to sight, seems to have achieved his perlocutionary goal of having the monarchs accept his transformation from foe to ally. Fernando and Isabel, for their part, serve as mediators of his individual political rebirth, just as they play a midwife role in the unification of Spain's diverse regions.

The monarchs next listen to the judge who is responsible for the torture of the townspeople. He admits that he has failed to gather any written evidence (2362-65). Then, surprisingly, the entire town of Fuente Ovejuna travels to Tordesillas. Their confession, though verbal only, provides evidence that could not be obtained in writing. This is typical of verbal confession, which often reveals information absent in written sources. Like the journey of Master Rodrigo, this trip is a pilgrimage similar to the return of a prodigal or a chosen people's trek to a promised land (Paolini 156).[23] The king allows the villagers an audience, and then interacts with them in a confessional, ritualistic framework. As with "Christian penitential practice in the early Church, [their] confession [is] communal and public" (Paolini 65). Bowing plays an important kinesthetic part in this political confession, much as it does in the religious sacrament. This collective obeisance may seem spontaneous but it, like rhetorical expression in general, is intentional, based on recognized conventions.[24]

When Isabel asks, "¿Los agresores son estos?" (2390), Mayor Esteban contritely responds, "Fuente Ovejuna, señora, / que humildes llegan agora / para serviros dispuestos" (2391-93). The mayor and others explain why they killed the *Comendador* and endeavor to obtain the king's clemency by persuading him of their innocence. Just as Flores had inadvertently confessed Fuente Ovejuna's sins before the town's arrival, so the collective protagonist now confesses those of Fernán Gómez. The mayor speaks of the tyranny of the *Comendador* while Frondoso and Mengo, kneeling along with the other villagers, corroborate the mayor's testimony (2394-2433).

Part of the religious confessional ritual involves a willingness on the part of the penitent to carry out the counsel of the confessor in exchange for absolution. According to Tentler, discipline and consolation are two constants in the long history of religious confession (*Sin and Confession* 13). Consistent with this tradition, the mayor expresses the collective disposition of his people to conform, to submit to any conditions that the sovereigns might impose (2434-41).[25] The penitent village receives the king's exculpation: "aunque fue grave el delito, / por fuerza ha de perdonarse" (2444-45).

The (non)confession of the villagers appears to support authoritarian national government (represented by the monarchs), as is expected in the contemporary political environment that Lope's drama depicts. It is not apparent whether the town's confession is accepted solely because no single criminal can be singled out for punishment, or if the monarchs are genuinely comfortable with the peasant's fight against tyranny. However, the sympathetic tone of the confessional ritual with the monarchs leaves the audience with a clear sense that Fernando and Isabel approve of what the villagers have done. Not only do the monarchs pardon the vassals from Fuente Ovejuna for killing their lord, but they also accept future responsibility for these vassals.

The final scene at Tordesillas—site of the famous 1494 Treaty that bears its name and a symbol of compromise and reconciliation—contrasts starkly with the earlier forced confessional episode. Here the confessors are not like the heartless Judge; they are powerful yet benign sovereigns, royal confessors who downplay justice to act as merciful doctors intent on healing patients. With the capacity to choose either the inquisitorial or pastoral role, they opt for the latter. At Tordesillas, even the traditional tension between "corte y aldea" finds resolution as villagers discover that the court of Fernando and Isabel reflects their own values. Far from being a center for slippery courtesans with Machiavellian values, the peasants find a place of refuge that sustains the traditional pastoral ideal: "una verdadera réplica del Edén, creado por Dios, donde reinan el amor y la armonía" (Rose 91-92).[26] Theirs is not a peace-seeking flight from court to countryside, but the reverse; nationalistic paradise is found in a unity-seeking pilgrimage from pastoral Fuente Ovejuna to courtly Tordesillas. The residence at Tordesillas becomes a secular cathedral, the nexus of political and spiritual authority to which villagers come of their own volition. As Erik Berggren argues in *The Psychology of Confession*, penitents seek to confess to someone whom they regard as possessing greater authority and power than themselves as they seek absolution (7). The Fuente Ovejuna confession, a bizarre mix of private and public, occurs in a private hearing before the Sovereigns, and yet a private confession in which the entire community participates is hardly confidential. Viewers of the drama are allowed to *see* and *hear* this confessional spectacle whereas they only *hear* the earlier confession-through-torture scene. In the forced confessional scene, the confessor travels to the people, attempts to extract a forced admission of guilt according to his own schedule and on his own terms, and fails. The episode at Tordesillas is an inversion of the confessional bout at Fuente Ovejuna. The penitents voluntarily make a pilgrimage to the site of trusted authority figures, openly admit what they have done, arrive on their own timetable, and succeed. Confession serves as a vehicle through which honorable villagers (presumably Old Christians) promote political unity, obtain royal favor, experience limited democracy, and find their niche in the burgeoning Spanish nation (Edward H. Friedman, "Sangre" 268). Collective penitence secures collective absolution. In the tradition of *deux ex machina*, a blend of the supernatural, the divine, and the miraculous characterizes the confluence of monarchical grace and collective confession that intervenes to rescue the villagers from their terrible dilemma (Cuddon, "deux ex machina"; A. Robert Lauer, "Rey" 260).

Lope's masterpiece is a seminal work in the development of the Spanish tragicomedy, which fuses two Greek literary traditions: the *tragedy* (focused on the upper class) and the *comedy* (concerned with the lower classes). In *Fuente Ovejuna*, he deals with both worlds, that of kings and *comendadores* (tragedy) and of common peasants (comedy). He sympathetically portrays lower class violence against a social superior, but does so in the context of loyalty to the monarchy (Cañadas 149-50). In the play, "a kidnapped, battered woman and a beaten, tortured man from the lowest order of the peasantry most dramatically represent the cause of the rebellion" (Cohen 327). In Act 3 the *Comendador* is called "tirano" seven times before he is killed (Robert Archer, "El pueblo, los reyes y el público: El pragmatismo dramático en *Fuente Ovejuna*" 111).[27] The tragic scenes of oppression, torture, and suffering are followed by those dominated by rejoicing and playful reminiscence (James A. Parr, "Tragicomedia" 307-09). In this drama, the confessional ritual provides the multifaceted catalyst that facilitates the blending of distinct literary genres, the harmonious interaction between upper and lower classes, the exculpation of common villagers by royal sovereigns, and the portrayal of torture scenes as both tragedy and comedy. Confession is an indispensable key that opens the door to our understanding of how Lope combines tragedy and comedy in *Fuente Ovejuna*.

The community's theatrical confession corresponds to the model of the *Festspiele* mentioned by Jorge Luis Borges: "[L]os *Festspiele* de Suiza [son] vastas y errantes representaciones teatrales, que requieren miles de actores y que reiteran episodios históricos en las mismas ciudades y montañas donde ocurrieron" ("Tema de traidor y del héroe" 149).[28] As in the Swiss model, the confessional pilgrimage of the people of Fuente Ovejuna is peripatetic, is performative, involves a large number of actors, and recounts an historical incident. It culminates in the *metaconfession* that frames Lope's memorable drama.[29] The final confession is a confession embedded within the larger confession made by the play in its entirety: all true Spaniards will confess their abandonment of regional loyalties and their adoption of the emerging nation personified by the Catholic Monarchs. The pilgrimage simultaneously pays homage to religious tradition and monarchical hegemony; it endorses the laws of God and man, and draws both into a cohesive whole. Wherever Lope's drama is performed, the stage becomes an artistic recreation of the historic town of Fuente Ovejuna, its text a reaffirmation of the national heritage of Catholic and monarchical Spain.

J. B. Hall is correct in asserting that Lope's *Fuente Ovejuna* is "a varied tale of treason, war, tyranny . . . murder and torture, with justice and love finally victorious" (*Lope de Vega: Fuente Ovejuna* 25). Hesse fittingly argues that the drama "represents a peak in the evolution of the Spanish theater in regard to its theme, character portrayal, the realism of its dialogue, and its dramatic execution" (17). What these and other writers might appropriately have added is that *Fuente Ovejuna* is also a tale of multiple confessions, of secular performative rituals that mimic the religious sacrament in order to promote Spanish nationhood, and a drama that reveals how confession is an eminently performative ritual, one that is both seen and heard.

Chapter Six

Confessing Incognito: Zorrilla's *Traidor, inconfeso y mártir*

Zorrilla's *Traidor, inconfeso y mártir* (1849)[1] is a complex confessional drama in which the dying confession of an enigmatic protagonist clashes with his earlier confession to the Pope. Zorrilla's drama contains multiple confessional scenes, complex confessional stagings, and both sacred and secular confessions. The play revolves around the mystery surrounding the disappearance of the Portuguese King, Don Sebastián, at the Battle of Alcazar (El-Ksar el Kebir), a conflict in which the Moors routed the Portuguese in 1578 (Bovill vii).[2] The discovery of personal identity through the confessional ritual is central to the plot, as is the role of the prison, or other confining space, as a breeding ground for confession. Each of the three major characters has a dual identity that is only resolved late in the play: the protagonist, the condemned "imposter" Gabriel[3] Espinosa reveals that he is really King Sebastián of Portugal; Aurora, the "daughter" he has raised, learns that she is actually the child of Rodrigo; and Rodrigo, the mayor, is jolted by the revelation that he is the father of the woman he desires to marry (Aurora).

Perhaps the most significant symbolic meaning accompanying the execution of King Sebastián at the end of Zorrilla's play is that confession leads to unification of the Iberian Peninsula. This Catholic confession serves to unravel a Romantic motif of dual identity. Thus the religious ritual, important to both Catholic Portugal and Catholic Spain, serves to bolster Spanish nationalism and imperialism. The King dies incognito, but his true identity is revealed by his written confession that is read only posthumously. It is this confession that not only unlocks the mystery of the protagonist's identity but also facilitates the way for Phillip II of Spain to extend his hegemony. While the monarch remains incognito, there is uncertainty as to whether Phillip's Portuguese counterpart and rival is still alive. Once confession illuminates the issue, the Spanish takeover is more easily justified. The Spanish King is now able to move into a political vacuum rather than take over a nation against the will of a ruling, and living, monarch.

Traidor, inconfeso y mártir is a playful confessional work that claims to unravel a mystery that is part of the cultural heritage of the Iberian Peninsula. Be-

uum rather than take over a nation against the will of a ruling, and living, monarch.

Traidor, inconfeso y mártir is a playful confessional work that claims to unravel a mystery that is part of the cultural heritage of the Iberian Peninsula. Behind the humor, the suspense, and the melodrama are serious messages about confession, nationalism, imperialism, fanaticism, identify, martyrdom, and the paradoxical nature of human life. Zorrilla's adroit artistic weaving of history and fabrication, of documented fact and unconfirmed legend, ultimately centers on the confessional message contained within a reliquary, a message that disentangles a Gordian knot of puzzling interpersonal relationships.

Consistent with Bakhtin's heteroglossia, it is critical to examine the work's historical background to capture the meaning of the drama. Don Sebastián's twenty-one-year rule as monarch stretches from 1557 to 1578. His father passes away only days before his birth while Joanna, his mother, deserts her son and returns to Spain. Catherine, Sebastián's grandmother and Joanna's aunt, rules in his stead, but the Spanish Catherine is despised by the Portuguese. Only two Portuguese males stand between Philip II, King of Spain, and the throne of neighboring Portugal: the infant Sebastián and Cardinal Henry, Sebastián's great uncle who removes himself as a barrier to Philip's succession when he vows to live a celibate life. The Portuguese Cardinal Henry does insist on being regent, but proves incompetent; meanwhile, the more competent Catherine returns to Spain (Bovill 7-8).

A Jesuit named Luiz da Camara and his brother, Martini Gonçalves da Camara, move to Lisbon during the regency of Catherine, Don Sebastián's grandmother. Luis has come from Tome to serve as Catherine's confessor and his brother Martini plays an important role in the Portuguese administration. After Catherine again leaves for Spain, the two brothers connive to drive the young man's great uncle, Cardinal Henry, out of power by declaring Don Sebastián capable to rule in his own right (although he is only fourteen years of age). The "rigorous clericalism" which marks his early formation produces a young ruler that is "a mystic and a fanatic who from childhood had visions of crusading triumphs" (Bovill 9). Zorrilla's fictional Don Sebastián reflects this zealous piety through his pilgrimages and quest for martyrdom. We might conjecture that his support for the killing of Protestants at the Saint Bartholomew's Day massacre is among the unnamed sins that he confesses to the Pope in *Traidor, inconfeso y mártir* (10).

Leading troops in northern Africa, Sebastián actively courts danger as he attempts to motivate his men with his foolhardy bravado: "He was ever in the *mêlée* and killing with his own sword, men afterwards said, as many Moors as any man in the army" (Bovill 136). This same sword, in Zorrilla's play, is important in the performative confession of the enigmatic protagonist, Gabriel Espinoza / Don Sebastián. His gradual confession is one of words, gestures, objects (sword and reliquary), and drama.

halló modo / de absolverme en su piedad" (80). The specifics of what Gabriel confesses to the Pope are not disclosed in Zorrilla's drama, but we may surmise that his high-ranking political stature, and his piracy, might justify such a high-level confession. The Pope was expected to assume original jurisdiction in certain cases. According to Tentler,

> among the sinners who need papal forgiveness are ... inquisitors who, defying justice and their consciences, fail to persecute heretics; people who aid the Saracens in the Holy Land; pirates especially excommunicated by the pope; and any great secular power—from Emperor to count—who gets himself or a close relative into the government of the city of Rome without the pope's permission. (*Sin and Confession* 306-07)

Bovill's history of the historical Sebastián's military exploits in northern Africa recounts how Sebastián, far outnumbered by his Moorish opponents, leaves Portugal, to the horror of his subjects. The populace is ordered to pray for his well-bring, which complement his mother Joanna's apprehensive dying words, "a prayer that her son would be restrained from crossing into Africa" (Bovill 14-15). Looking for a fight with the Moors, he finds one; fortuitously he reaches Tangier still alive, and then returns to Portugal. In the midst of bitter opposition and sycophantic support, King Sebastián forges an alliance with Mulai Mohammed, a deposed African sultan who longs to regain power. If all goes well, both will rise politically; the Islamic Mulai Mohammed will reclaim his throne, and the Christian Sebastián will become Morocco's emperor. Power, not religious toleration, lies at the heart of the African's alliance with the aspiring Portuguese leader; he is "an implacable hater of Christians whom he treated brutally whenever they had the misfortune to fall into his hands" (Bovill 16, 23). Philip II is on favorable terms with Mulai Mohammed's uncle, the legitimate ruler (Abd el-Malek), and tries to avoid an African imbroglio. Mulai Mohammed is, consequently, *persona non grata* in Spain, but not so with the Portuguese monarch. With implausible irony, Sebastián welcomes the opportunity to join forces with the Islamic torturer of Christians in order to pursue his dream of fighting the Moors under the banner of Christianity. Apparently untroubled by the inconsistency, Sebastián welcomes Mohammed, his son, and six hundred followers to Portuguese Tangier, where they await Sebastián and the troops he plans to bring to that location (24). Such collaboration with a known enemy of Christianity may well be a matter serious enough to warrant confession to the Pope.

Zorrilla's mid-nineteenth-century Spanish audiences, if aware of the history surrounding the controversial Sebastián, may have made a mental connection between his confession to the Pope and his pro-Muslim alliance with the cruel Mulai Mohammed. Such a partnership is not only a matter of religious concern but also a disconcerting political concern, for "Christian soldiers of fortune and other adventurers ... had sought service under the sultans" (Bovill 26) in northern Africa. Moreover, among the Europeans who had become the captives of

Zorrilla's mid-nineteenth-century Spanish audiences, if aware of the history surrounding the controversial Sebastián, may have made a mental connection between his confession to the Pope and his pro-Muslim alliance with the cruel Mulai Mohammed. Such a partnership is not only a matter of religious concern but also a disconcerting political concern, for "Christian soldiers of fortune and other adventurers . . . had sought service under the sultans" (Bovill 26) in northern Africa. Moreover, among the Europeans who had become the captives of pirates, "many had apostatized [from Catholicism], married local women and settled down permanently in the country as freemen" (26).

The subjugation of the last Moorish stronghold at Granada in 1492 occurred during the reign of the Catholic Monarchs, Ferdinand of Aragon and Isabella of Castile. It is common knowledge that this victory brings to a close the centuries-old *Reconquista* in Spain. Less widely recognized is Isabella's religious passion for defeating the Moors in northern Africa. Ferdinand's enthusiasm for the endeavor grows in response to his "concern at the growing menace of African corsair raids on the shores of Spain" (Bovill 1). Thus the issue of pirates, important in Zorrilla's drama, looms large in international affairs—in the Mediterranean, the Caribbean and elsewhere—long before Sebastián's time. After Philip II ascends the Spanish throne in 1555, piracy continues to plague his nation and empire. In the name of Christianity, he opposes "the infidel raiders who were not only sacking towns and villages and enslaving thousands of his Spanish and Italian subjects but even waylaying his rich galleons returning from the Americas" (2).

Sebastián meets his uncle, Philip II, at Guadalupe to discuss joint cooperation in northern Africa. Philip first fails to convince his nephew of the futility of an African enterprise, and then fails to persuade him not to risk his own life in the venture. Zorrilla captures this illogical penchant for personal glory via martyrdom in the title and the plot of his drama. For Sebastián to lose his crown, he must lose his life. This not only makes for intriguing drama, but also supports the cause of Spanish nationalism, since the Portuguese king's death opens the way for Spanish domination of both Iberian nations. The historical record indicates that Philip reluctantly agrees to send troops and galleys in support of Sebastián's bold scheme. Meanwhile, in a bid for Spanish friendship, Mulai Mohammed's uncle (Abd el-Malek) offers to curtail anti-Spanish corsair activity, pledging to hang pirates who seize Spanish prizes. Philip still hopes to escape participation with Sebastián when the time for action finally arrives (Bovill 53-61).

The Duke of Alva, the Spanish monarch's belligerent chief advisor, wants an even larger Spanish commitment, and urges that Spain fulfill its commitment (Bovill 60-1). When, as Alva fears, Philip withdraws Spanish support, his nephew decides that Portugal will continue alone. Although Spanish aid has been withdrawn, Pope Gregory XIII extends his papal blessing to the enterprise.[4] In addition to the pontiff's blessing, "the coveted bull of the Holy Crusade"

eggs and milk during Lent and meat on certain fasts" (71). The monarchs of both Spain and Portugal secure the Vatican's authorization to transform this religious privilege into a profitable venture. With Rome's approval they not only sell the right to drink milk and eat eggs during specified holy days, but also to *require* their purchase. Because permission to compel the purchase of these dairy products is extended to every part of the far-flung Portuguese and Spanish empires, the economic desirability of finding Moors to persecute becomes a matter of national foreign policy (60-1, 70-1).

Sebastián is genuinely interested in defending the faith by tormenting Moors and regaining the *Cruzada*, which has not been renewed in recent years. Consequently, when the Pope restores the privilege and blesses Sebastián's African expedition, it gives the venture added credibility and resources (Bovill 71). Sebastián's confession to the Pope, as depicted in *Traidor, inconfeso y mártir*, should be viewed against the historical backdrop of a vibrant religious and economic relationship between Roman Tiara and Portuguese Crown. In Zorrilla's drama, as in real life, Sebastián's world is one of popes, pirates, and profits.

When Sebastián's ill-prepared expedition finally sails, it includes mostly Portuguese (about 10,000) but also Germans (3,000) and Castilians (2,000) that Philip has allowed. The Vatican's support is clearly visible: the Pontiff not only sends 600 troops, but also a legate delivers the *Cruzada*, and over 1,000 Portuguese clerics accompany the expedition (Bovill 85-7). Sebastián predictably takes inadequate caution for his own safety—"his was the blind courage of the fanatic" (Bovill 96)—a characteristic Zorrilla's underscores through his protagonist's quest for martyrdom. Prior to his own demise in battle, with typical fanaticism, Sebastián seeks "to inspire his troops to superhuman efforts by his readiness to hazard his own life" (131). As Bovill argues, "we may be sure that he gloried in the spilling of his royal blood" (131). When his horse is killed, he is seen mounting another one; nor does a slightly injured right arm prove a deterrent to further action (131).

In the heat of battle, Sebastián is lost from sight. Nobles and body-guards hunt for him in vain. Meanwhile, the Moors win the battle of El-Ksar el-Kebir in just six hours, a quarter-day that changes the history of Portugal, Spain, and their far-flung empires. With Sebastián removed from the imperial picture, Portugal soon comes under the Spanish crown and Philip II of Spain now doubles as Philip I of Portugal. After the battle, the Moors desire to take a live Sebastián captive, for his tremendous ransom potential, but he appears to have been killed by a Moor who does not know the regal status of his opponent. (In Zorrilla's play, likewise, the dying protagonist is executed by those who do not know for certain his true identity.) Even the king's dead body could have brought money to the Moors, but after it is found, they refuse to surrender it to the Portuguese, even for 10,000 ducats, and Sebastián is buried in an unknown grave in El-Ksar el-Kebir. Later, through Philip II's mediation, the martyr's remains are transferred to a Belem church. Mulai Muhammed's body is also later found. Because he, his uncle (the Shereef), and Sebastián all die during the brief six-hour inter-

captive, for his tremendous ransom potential, but he appears to have been killed by a Moor who does not know the regal status of his opponent. (In Zorrilla's play, likewise, the dying protagonist is executed by those who do not know for certain his true identity.) Even the king's dead body could have brought money to the Moors, but after it is found, they refuse to surrender it to the Portuguese, even for 10,000 ducats, and Sebastián is buried in an unknown grave in El-Ksar el-Kebir. Later, through Philip II's mediation, the martyr's remains are transferred to a Belem church. Mulai Muhammed's body is also later found. Because he, his uncle (the Shereef), and Sebastián all die during the brief six-hour interval, the conflict is sometimes called "the battle of the Three Kings," a struggle in which the Papal Nuncio also perishes (Bovill 137, 139, 141, 155, 142).

An intriguing, albeit foolish, spin-off of the history-changing battle of El-Ksar, which facilitates Spain's acquisition of Portugal from 1580 to 1640, is the rise of the *sebastianistas*, a sect that rejects the tradition that Sebastián's body was ever transferred from Moorish hands in Africa to the Portuguese. They refuse to believe that the body buried in a Belem church is truly that of the impetuous monarch. Moreover, a wounded Portuguese noble further promote the *sebastianista* cause when he travels to Tangier and audaciously claims to be King Sebastián. Meanwhile, in France an account circulates that claims the Portuguese King has not been killed but merely taken captive and that another body lies buried in Belem. The rumor mill also spreads the news that Sebastián has left the battle to gain refuge with the legendary Christian prince Prestor John or that he had gone to Persia (Bovill 155-6). This type of speculation helps lay the cultural foundations for Zorrilla's drama.

In *Traidor, inconfeso y mártir*, to ease Gabriel's tormented conscience and thoughts, the Pope instructs him to do penance by making a pilgrimage on foot to the Holy Sepulcher. He completes this arduous talk and also complies with another drastic penitential requirement: to renounce both his title and his name.[5] He returns to the sea, this time not as a pirate, and ends up taking custody of Aurora (Rodrigo's daughter), who is about to be sold as a slave. Gabriel desires to return her to her father, who has not raised her, and now fails to recognize her to such an extent that he desires to marry her. It is Gabriel she wishes to marry, regardless of who he really is, whether king or imposter, but Gabriel refuses. At one point Aurora presses Gabriel, "Dime quién soy: dime quién eres" (99), but not until he is on the verge of martyrdom does the Portuguese king reveal the truth about her identity and that of her father Rodrigo.

Zorrilla's drama includes both a love triangle and a triangle of confession. Each of the three primary characters serves as confessor and confessant to the other two, and each completes a pilgrimage of self-discovery that ends successfully, following a labyrinth of confessions, with the sacrifice of the innocent Gabriel, who dies like a paschal lamb. Gabriel argues that he must die as a sacrificial martyr, whether impostor or king, for the good of the Spanish people (140). Demonstrating masterful control over the confessional process, he ap-

that often characterizes confession. The imposter Gabriel must die so that the true identity of King Sebastián may be born. Moreover, Gabriel gives his life so that a new unified Iberian nation may flourish under the intensely Catholic Phillip. Zorrilla deconstructs, as it were, the process of ritualistic confession, for if Gabriel (a name suggesting divinity) confesses prior to his death, he becomes less religious, violates his obligation as a penitent (that derives from his previous verbal confession to the Pope), and risks losing his previous absolution. Confession threatens confession, but the message in the dying protagonist's *relicario*, like a miraculous holy relic, breaks the impasse. Through it, Gabriel-Sebastián emerges as a type of confessor himself by threatening with "pena de excomunión" (145) anyone (including a *sacerdote*) who does not burn this written confession. His note shatters the confessional monopoly of the clergy by demonstrating his willingness to confess to anyone who happens to read it: "Quien quier que fueres"(145).

Not only Gabriel—"aquel embozado incógnito" (23), "ese personaje / misterioso" (25)—but also the other two confessants are each, in a sense, *incognito* and *misterioso*, and each seeks self-knowledge through a complex confessional maze. The lynchpin to this confessional complex is the final note, which allows Gabriel to die impostor and king, hero and villain, confessor and penitent, angel and devil, Christian and pagan, *confeso* and *inconfeso*.

Chapter Seven

Confessional Literature: Redefining a Genre

Much of the appeal of confessional literature lies in the pervasiveness of confessional rituals. Historical circumstances of authors and their audiences change over time, as does the penitential ritual itself. The specific crises that prompt confessional activity vary widely, but the human tendency to seek liberation from personal and collective crises through confession persists. The revelation of private inner thoughts and experiences helps individuals and groups unburden themselves and share weighty loads. Confession typically involves a quest for self-discovery, which facilitates personal transformation. Confessional literature is a literature of communication. Penitents not only confess *about* something but *to* someone.

Confessions are always performative. They contain kinesthetic elements and involve hegemonic power relationships in which penitents submit to the control of their confessors, and the institutions they represent, out of self-interest. Each confession is a rhetorical speech act with perlocutionary potential. Bakhtin's heteroglossia, which seeks to explain how non-linguistic factors influence the meaning of verbal expressions, helps us more fully understand any confessional interaction.

Critical writing about confessional literature has routinely categorized it as a subcategory of autobiography but, as this book demonstrates, such a notion is limiting and misleading. The confessional genre, an independent genre of liberation, needs to be freed itself from such conceptual limitations. Confessional literature holds timeless value and fascination because it connects with real human needs and emotions. Like great literature generally, it communicates issues that are intensely human and ageless in their appeal. When confession is analyzed in the light of speech-act theory, rhetorical tradition, hegemonic theory, and Bakhtin's "living heteroglossia," it becomes evident that confessants and their interlocutors not only *speak* but also *act*. Confession may be either a sacred *or* a secular sacrament, a performative ritual directed by those believed to hold ecclesiastical keys *or* by those making no such claim. Confession is born of crisis, and is an expression that helps confessants cope, while pursuing a journey of self-discovery, a journey that is always rooted in community. Confession is a perlocutionary activity in which a confessant seeks to persuade a confessor and engages the confessor in a truly symbiotic relationship. Confessional writing is a highly reflective and transformational activity in which death-rebirth and light-darkness motifs are common.

The foremost thrust of the new theoretical model presented in this book is not to maintain that previous authors and critics have erred in their interpretations but rather to insist that they have not gone far enough. Earlier theorists accurately stress the religious foundations of confession, appreciate its relationship to crisis, acknowledge its persistent tie to community, emphasize self-discovery as a fundamental characteristic, understand the crucial role of the interlocutor, and perceive the importance of the birth-death motif. Each of these confessional characteristics relates to classical rhetoric, and in particular to the key role that performance plays in persuading others. This new model invites a rereading of Spanish texts, even those that are widely known. Such Spanish literary luminaries as Cervantes, Lope de Vega, Zorrilla, and Unamuno have made important contributions to confessional literature, although they are not generally considered to be authors of confessional texts. While some books have confessional frames, more common are literary works with embedded confessional activity.

Bakhtin's theory of "heteroglossia," which emphasizes how nonverbal forces shape the meaning of verbal utterances, is a powerful theoretical concept because of its comprehensiveness. Heteroglossia urges us to explore the nuances and hidden meanings of confessional utterances. This book uses "living heteroglossia" (Bakhtin 668) as an overarching umbrella to unify the various theoretical strands that contribute to its overall theoretical construct. Speech act theory blends well with Bakhtin's theory of heteroglossia. Confessional interchanges commonly include indirect speech acts, complex statements such as those with double meanings, or expressions that are ironic or metaphoric. A confessant's statement of guilt may double, for example, as a plea for absolution. Speech acts move beyond the verbal and enter the realm of the performative. They take on a life of their own and cause things to happen. As with speech generally, confessional expression acquires meaning only through context. Power relationships, including hegemonic struggles, are part of the perlocutionary confessional ritual. Typically, the confessor-interlocutor not only assumes the dominant position in this power relationship but also plays the role of a midwife in giving birth to a confession.

Both confessional frames and embedded scenes generally imitate the religious sacrament of penance. Confessional literature is a flexible genre. *Don Quijote*, a little recognized confessional novel, has many confessional scenes embedded within its overall confessional frame. Although much of Cervantes' classic is a third-person narrative, "La historia del cautivo" assumes an autobiographical form. Gutiérrez's *Cornelia Bororquia* is an epistolary novel in which private letters give accounts of confessional scenes in a polyphonic structure that goes beyond autobiography. In Unamuno's *San Manuel Bueno, mártir*, the confessing narrator reveals the confessions of others as well as her own. Sender's *Réquiem por un campesino español* utilizes a third-person viewpoint to present two parallel confessions, one in prose and one in poetry. Although confession and autobiography are often combined, each can exist without the other.

Although the theoretical model proposed in this book applies to all genres, drama is inherently performative and helps us recognize the nonverbal qualities of the confessional ritual. Lope de Vega's Golden Age masterpiece *Fuente Ovejuna*, is a highly confessional work, yet the extensive body of literary criticism about the drama has failed to adequately consider its abundant confessional scenes. Zorrilla's nineteenth-century work *Traidor, inconfeso y mártir* has not hitherto been classified as a confessional work, although confession is central to its plot development and is reflected in its title.

Confessional literature stretches beyond works of drama and overlaps every literary genre; it is a varied, fascinating, timeless, and vital genre; it is eminently dramatic, and always performative; it is a hopeful crying out in response to crisis; it is a plea for reconciliation with community; it tells of confessional martyrs such as Gutiérrez's Cornelia Bororquia, Zorrilla's don Sebastián, and Unamuno's san Manuel Bueno; it reveals the liberty-seeking dreams of Cervantes' Zoraida-María and Sender's Paco el del Molino; it is performed on stages as varied as the priestly confessional, the confining prison, and the running board of an automobile; its boundless geographic reach extends to such places as Valverde de Lucerna, the northern coast of Africa, and the royal residence at Tordesillas; it is an individual's private admission of guilt or a community's open plea for mercy; it is auricular-ocular confession, a pervasive
human activity that is both *heard* and *seen*.

Notes

Chapter One

1. See, for instance, Peter M. Axthelm, *The Modern Confessional Novel* (1967); Terrence Doody, *Confession and Community in the Novel* (1980); John R. Rosenberg, *The Circular Pilgrimage and Anatomy of Confessional Autobiography in Spain* (1994); and Susan M. Levin, *The Romantic Art of Confession* (1998). See my "Unfettering Confession: Ritualized Performance in Spanish Narrative and Drama" (2005) for English translations of works covered in this book, for a more comprehensive bibliography of sources, and for additional discussion of Spanish confessional works.

2. See also her later work, *The Romantic Art of Confession: DeQuincey, Musset, Sand, Lamb, Hogg, Frémy, Soulié, Janin* (1998).

3. See Otger Steggink, ed., "Introduction" to *Libro de la vida* (1986); Rhodes, "What's in a Name: On Teresa of Ávila's *Book*" (2000) 85-6.

4. For a more detailed look at the rhetorical and performative nature of confessional literature, see my "Unfettering Confession: Ritualized Performance in Spanish Narrative and Drama" (2005) and "Forced Political Confession: Buero Vallejo's *El sueño de la razón*" (2006).

5. A modification of the original 1943 edition is *La confesión: género literario* (1995).

Chapter Two

1. Rendered *raznorecie* in the original Russian, the English translation is based on the combination of two Greek words: *hetero*, meaning different or other; and *glossa*, meaning tongue (J. A. Cuddon, *The Penguin Dictionary of Literary Terms and Literary Theory* (1998) "Heteroglossia").

2. The link between performative communication and wearing a mask, either literally or figuratively, is of ancient origin. In Greek theater, actors routinely wore a *persona*: "a mask or false face of clay or bark" (Cuddon, "Persona"). From this word have emerged *dramatis personae* and *person*.

3. In the Dutch Reformed Church, public confession was required for reconciliation with the community of the faithful well into the seventeenth century. However, as the Church matured and grew in numbers, "sin and confession became more of a private personal concern and much less of a matter to be brought before the religious community" (Charles H. Parker, "The Rituals of Reconciliation: Admonition, Confession and Community in the Dutch Reformed Church" (2000) 115).

4. "The glossary in Bakhtin's *The Dialogic Imagination* notes that heteroglossia is determined contextually and extra-linguistically as well as intra-linguistically: 'all utterances are heteroglot in that they are functions of a matrix of forces practically impossible to recoup'" (Jeremy Hawthorne, *A Glossary of Contemporary Literary Theory* (1992) "Heteroglossia").

5. Hannah Arendt maintains that "from the outset in formal philosophy, thinking has been thought of in terms of *seeing*" (*The Life of the Mind: Thinking* (1971) 110; italics in original).

Chapter Three

1. I have used *DQ* as the abbreviation for *Don Quijote de la Mancha* (2000) [1605, 1615]. In this chapter's discussion of "La historia del cautivo," parenthetical references with only a page number refer to the *Quijote*. For additional interpretive analysis about the *Quijote* and confession, see my "The Confessant of La Mancha: Don Quixote's Personal and National Pilgrimage" (2007) 103-17.

2. According to María Antonia Garcés, "'La historia del cautivo' provides a clear résumé of Cervantes' military career in the Mediterranean followed by an extraordinary depiction of captivity in Barbary" (*Cervantes in Algiers: A Captive's Tale* (2002) 185).

3. Both wine and blood are important symbolic elements in Catholic worship. Whether intentional or not, their placement before *el cautivo*'s confessional tale involving themes of Christian conversion and liberation seems fortuitous.

4. *Lela* translates as *señora* in Arabic (*DQ* 407 Note 9).

5. The Biblical account after which Cervantes patterns his narrative is the classic account of the birth of Jesus (Luke 2: 4-7, King James Version).

6. "This perception of the Virgin, adorned with gold, pearls, and priceless gems, was especially popular in the Spain of the Counter-Reformation" (Garcés 214).

7. Action regarding the liberation of *el cautivo*, Zoraida, and others takes place on Thursday and Friday, the traditional days of Jesus' experience at the Garden of Gethsemane (Thursday), and on the cross (Friday) (*DQ* 430, 434).

8. Garcés provides an excellent description of Cervantes' captivity and escape attempts (38-59).

Chapter Four

1. I deal with this same imagery in my "Forced Political Confession: Buero Vallejo's *El sueño de la razón*" (2006) 129-43. Rueda discusses the spider web symbolism in *Cartas sin lacrar: La novela epistolar y la España Ilustrada, 1789-1840.* (2001) 312.

2. In references to *San Manuel Bueno, mártir*, the abbreviation *SMBM* will be used, or simply the page number where unambiguous. An English translation is Anthony Kerrigan trans. and intro., (1956) 207-67. The Spanish version used in this study is Unamuno, *San Manuel Bueno, mártir* (1979).

3. A *promoter fideis* carefully examines the validity of evidence used in the support of beatification (Andrachuk, "'He That Eateth of This Bread Shall Live Forever' (John 6:58): Lázaro's Communion" (1991) 207 note 3).

4. For a discussion of speech acts and mental states, see Wolfgang Motsch, "Situational Context and Illocutionary Force" (1980) 158.

5. Colbert I. Nepaulsingh explains that "one of the most important elements of the evangelical tradition is the mysterious nature of the transmission of the text, and of the insertion by the author of himself into the text" ("In Search of a Tradition, not a Source, for *San Manuel Bueno, mártir*" (1987) 327).

6. All parenthetical page listings are from *Réquiem por un campesino español* (1994) [1950], which has been translated into English by Elinor Randall as *Requiem for a Spanish Peasant* (1960).

7. The term "duque" (duke) conjures up images of fascist leadership; the Italian fascist leader Mussolini was known as "il duce" (the leader). Hitler and Franco played comparable fascist roles in Germany and Spain respectively.

Chapter Five

1. This chapter is based on my previously published article "'Es de Lope": The Drama of Confession and *Fuente Ovejuna*" (2007).

2. "Almost single-handed[ly] he created a national theatre" (John Garrett Underhill, "Introduction" *Four Plays of Lope de Vega* (1936) viii). Citations from the play *Fuente Ovejuna* are based on the Francisco López Estrada edition (1996).

3. An approximate publication date of 1610-1615 is given in Núria Roig Fisas y Bienvenido Morros, eds., *El mejor alcalde, el rey* (1989) 26.

4. Lope gained acceptance from the Inquisition to the point of becoming an inquisitorial judge himself (Francis C. Hayes, *Lope de Vega* (1967) 21).

5. Lope placed great personal emphasis on confession. Although told by one priest, who tired of his confessions, to obtain a new confessor, Lope typically confessed weekly. In his later years, he lashed himself until the blood flowed (Hayes 21). Lope was deeply committed to his form of zealous repentance (Francisco Icaza, *Lope de Vega: Sus amores y sus odios, y otros estudios* (1962) 140-43). In 1614 he was ordained a priest: "I left worldly vanities and was ordained, for it was necessary to bring order into my disorder" (cited by Hugo Albert Rennert, *The Life of Lope de Vega (1562-1635)* (1968) 211).

6. Lope, more than any other Golden Age Spanish dramatist, drew inspiration from historical events, but felt very free to take artistic liberty with the past (Carol Bingham Kirby, "Historia" (2002) 165; Charles Vincent Aubrun, *La comedia española, 1600-1680* (1968) 250). An historical account supplies the basic plot for Lope's drama: Fray Francisco de Rades y Andrada, *Crónica de la Orden de Calatrava* (1572). This sixteenth century work recounts the brutality of the villagers towards Fernán Gómez; it has a far more negative tone than the heroic role granted the villagers in Lope's drama (79-80). An accessible transcript of relevant excerpts from this source is found in Blecua's "Introduction" to his edition of *Peribañez* y *Fuente Ovejuna* (1981) 36-40; an English translation is found in Spitzer (1988) 417-18n.

7. The Fourth Lateran Council required that "All the faithful of either sex, after they have reached the age of discernment, should individually confess all their sins in a faithful manner to their own priest at least once a year." Failure to do so could bring stern penalties: "Otherwise they shall be barred from entering a church during their lifetime and they shall be denied a christian burial at death." The priest, a "skilled doctor," cares for the "the wounds of the injured one" ("Fourth Lateran Council—1215 A.D.")

8. Fernando and Isabel were always depicted positively in Lope's dramas (Hayes 70).

9. The official documents that emerged from the Fourteenth Session of the Council of Trent explained that "the entire confession of sins was . . . instituted by the Lord" and that when he was "about to ascend from earth to heaven, [he] left priests[,] His own vicars, as presidents and judges," with responsibility to "pronounce the sentence of forgiveness or retention of sins." The people were admonished not to hide their sins from the priest-physician: "they who act otherwise, and knowingly keep back certain sins" could not be forgiven "for if the sick be ashamed to show his wound to the physician, his medical art cures not that which it knows not of." The Council stated that confession was to be secret and "to a priest alone," that public confession, though not specifically forbidden, had never been "commanded by a divine precept." As to frequency, Catholics were to confess "at least once a year," preferably during "that most sacred and most acceptable time of Lent,—a custom which this holy Synod most highly approves of and embraces, as pious and worthy of being retained" ("The Council of Trent").

10. According to Thomas N. Tentler, the Counter-Reformation promoted "the use of the confessional box" and launched "a massive campaign to increase the frequency of confession" ("Postscript" (2000) 248).

11. The Orders of Calatrava, Alcántara, and Santiago were the three leading military orders of the day. According to Rades y Andrada, the Order of Calatrava was established in 1158 AD. Particularly relevant pages are 6-7, 11-12, 77-83. Fighting Moors permeates the book (e.g., 13, 19, 37, 57). For a *Comendador* to fight villagers who are presumably Old Christians is directly contrary to the traditional mission of the Order. *Comendador* may be translated as *Knight-Commander* or simply *Commander*.

12. Peter N. Dunn links honor to heredity and social status, and honra to reputation, which is dependent on the perceptions of others (166). In *Los comendadores de Córdoba*, Lope explains, "Honra es aquella que consiste en otro; / ningún hombre es honrado por sí mismo, / que del otro recibe honra un hombre; . . ." (cited by Dunn, "Honor/Honra" (2002) 166).

13. He can aptly be compared to Nero and Heliogabalus, two infamous Roman leaders whose names have become metaphors for cruel and unjust leadership: "perverso Nerón" (2422) "Heliogábalo dirás, / más que una fiera, inhumano" (1175-76). Wilson's *Arte of Rhetorique* (1909) [1553], which gives us numerous insights into the rhetorical practices of the early modern era, recommends the metaphoric use of Heliogabalus as a symbol of a depraved man (14) and Nero as the worst of leaders, a tyrant who "wanted no good counsaile, and such a Master he had, as never any had the better, and yet what one alive was worse then he?" (79). The *Comendador* fits both rhetorical images; like Heliogabalus, he is immoral; like Nero, he is unwilling to heed counsel and is the worst of all characters in *Fuente Ovejuna*. Brewer (*Brewer's Dictionary of Phrase and Fable* (1981) [1817]) states that "Varius Avitus Bassinius (205-22) who became Roman emperor as Marcus Aurelius Antoninus (218-22) was called Elagabalus [Heliogabalus] because he had been a high priest of the sun-god at Emesa. His brief reign was marked by unparalleled debaucheries, cruelties, and loathsome practices. He and his mother were slain by the Praetorian Guard" (Evans, "Elagabalus"). Under "Nero," Brewer states: "Any bloody-minded man, relentless tyrant, or evil-doer or extraordinary cruelty; from the depraved and infamous Roman Emperor, C. Claudius Nero (AD 37, 54-68).

14. The *Comendador's* "gallows sorrow," motivated by fear rather than internal transformation, prompts a shallow and self-serving confession, the type that Tentler describes as the superficial grief "experienced by the thief, about to face execution, who hates his punishment but not his crime" (*Sin and Confession* (1977) 351).

15. Wilson comments on the rhetorical value of humor in difficult circumstances (104). According to Henry K. Ziomek, "The *gracioso*, an indispensable character in the comedia . . . emerged as a stock figure in the hands of Lope de Vega" and ". . . the *gracioso* is unconditionally loyal" (*A History of Spanish Golden Age Drama* (1984) 46). Lope deals with serious themes, but does so "con la sonrisa en los labios" (José F. Montesinos, *Estudios sobre Lope de Vega* (1967) 7). For further discussion of the gracioso in the literature of Lope, see "La figura del donaire o el gracioso" in Alfonso Noriega Cantú, *El humorismo en la obra de Lope de Vega* (1976) 109-28, and Susana Hernández Araico, "Gracioso" (2002) 160-62. Lope "invented the *gracioso*, the clown who usually parodied the actions of his master and provided the comic relief" (Everett W. Hesse, *The Comedia and Points of View* (1984) 10).

16. The royal acceptance of the collective confession implies not only a rejection of the tyrannical leadership of Fernán Gómez, but also a repudiation of the corrupt Order and practices he personifies. The Order of Calatrava has opposed the rule of Isabel (sister

to King Enrique IV, whose death is followed by a civil war over the right of succession) and supported the claims to the throne of Juana, the deceased king's "daughter." Juana, Isabel's rival, is disparagingly dubbed "La Beltraneja" because of her suspected illegitimacy (as the daughter of Beltrán de la Cueva rather than Enrique IV). Alfonso V also sought to bring Castille under Portuguese rule (Alberto Castilla, "Conflictos sociales" (2002) 85). The Order's support for Juana is deemed traitorous by the Catholic Monarchs. For a summary of the succession controversy and Lope's use of the writings of Rades y Andrada, see Ricardo E. Alegría, "El grito de 'Fuente Ovejuna lo hizo' en Puerto Rico en 1542, tres cuartos de siglo, antes de Lope de Vega escribir su comedia" (1990) 86-87.

17. Anne T. Thayer pursues these roles of the confessor in her "Judge and Doctor: Images of the Confessor in Printed Model Sermon Collections, 1450-1520" (2000).

18. ". . . we must recall again the two functions of the institutions of forgiveness that occupy our attention: consolation and discipline" (Thomas N. Tentler, *Sin and Confession* (1977) 234).

19. García Pavón (1967) argues that the actual popular rebellion in April 1476, upon which Lope based his drama, was likely not based on a unanimous decision by the community (13).

20. Susan L. Fischer deals with the relationship between Foucault's thought and *Fuente Ovejuna* ("Fuente Ovejuna on the Rack: Interrogation of a Carnivalesque Theater of Terror" (1997) 61-63).

21. By persuading the young Maestre to assist "him in his plan of treason at Ciudad Real," the *Comendador* "has threatened the unity of the whole kingdom. He has no moral right to foment sedition against the monarchy, which has the right to a peaceful and orderly existence" (Robert L. Fiore, *Drama and Ethos: Natural-Law Ethics in Spanish Golden Age Theater* (1975) 16).

22. I am indebted to Dr. Aaron M. Kahn for pointing out the shepherd-sheep-wolf motif.

23. "The journey or return to Divine grace from the state of sin is figured in the journey of the Prodigal Son back to his Father, in the Exodus of the Israelites to the Promised Land, and in metaphors of ship and sea-voyages. The purpose of the journey is the conversion of the will from the state of sin to grace" (Paolini 156). Paolini's 1973 dissertation, used in this study, was later adapted and published as *Confessions of Sin and Love in the Middle Ages* (Lanham, MD: UP of America, 1982).

24. According to Wilson, rhetoric in general is learned and not natural: "Rhetorique is an Arte to set foorth by utteraunce of words, matter at large, or (as *Cicero* doth say) it is a learned, or rather an artificiall declaration of the mynd, in the handling of any cause, called in contentin, that may through reason largely be discussed" (Wilson 1). According to Gilbert Austin, Buffon argues that kneeling is one of many gestures that occur so rapidly that they seem to be involuntary, but in reality, are not: "we are deceived by the effect of habit; for they depend upon reflection, and are rather to be considered as proofs of the perfection of the mechanism of the human body, from the promptitude with which all the members obey the commands of the will" (cited by Austin, *Chironomia or A Treatise on Rhetorical Delivery* (1966) [1806], 485-86).

25. This conformity on the part of the villagers corresponds to Lope's personal philosophy; Amado Alonso calls Lope "el más grande poeta de la conformidad" (cited by Castilla 86).

26. See also Escudero Baztán, "Villanos" (2002) 317-18.

27. The historical account of Rades y Andrada does not use the term *tirano* at all.

Some sixteenth century Spanish theologians interpreted Thomas of Aquinas in a way that justified not only resistance to a tyrannical leader but even his death at the hands of an offended populace (Robert Archer, "El pueblo, los reyes y el público: El pragmatismo dramático en *Fuente Ovejuna*" (1990) 111-12; Hesse, *The Comedia and Points of View* (1984) 81n).

28. See my "Borges juega con la literatura confesional" (2004).

29. My use of the term *metaconfession* is inspired by the concept of *metatheatre*, which derives from Lionel Abel, *Metatheatre: A New View of Dramatic Form* (1963); see Catherine Larson, "Metatheater and the Comedia: Past, Present, and Future" (1994) 211-14; Hesse (1984) 54n.

Chapter Six

1. Only recently has this work been translated into English, although it is unclear whether the translation has been published. According to a 15 April 2004 Westminster College announcement titled "Theatre Westminster Presents 'Baker from Madrigal,'" Zorrilla's drama was translated by Dr. Jeff Bersett for a campus performance in Wilmington, Pennsylvania. (http://www.westminster.edu/news/releases/release.cfm?id= 75). A more literal translation of the title would be "*The Unconfessed Traitor and Martyr.*"

2. For additional information on the myth-shrouded controversy that surrounds the death of Don Sebastián at the battle Alcazar, see João José Alves Dias, *Portugal do Renascimento à Crise Dinástica* (1987), James M. Anderson, *The History of Portugal* (2000), Sabine Baring-Gould, *Curious Myths of the Middle Ages* (1867), E. W. Bovill, *The Battle of Alcazar: An Account of the Defeat of Don Sebastián of Portugal of El-Ksar el-Kebir* (1952), John Fiske, *Myths and Myth-Makers: Old Tales and Superstitions Interpreted by Comparative Mythology* (1902), Antonio Rodriguez-Moñino, *Viaje a España del Rey Don Sebastián de Portugal (1576-1577)* (1956), William Spencer, *Historical Dictionary of Morocco* (1980), and Dahiru Yahya, *Morocco in the Sixteenth Century: Problems and Patterns in African Foreign Policy* (1981).

3. "Gabriel" means "man of God" (*Brewer's Dictionary of Phrase and Fable*, "Gabriel").

4. Gregory was pope from 1572 to 1585. The papal years of his successors are Sixtus V (1585 to 1590), Urban VII (1590), Gregory XVI (1590-1591), Innocent XI (1591), and Clement VIII (1592-1605).

5. "According to the medieval theology of penance, a sinner must not only be absolved from his guilt but must also pay for his sins in the form of some kind of punishment" (Thomas N. Tentler, *Sin and Confession* (1977) 318).

Bibliography

Abel, Lionel. *Metatheatre: A New View of Dramatic Form*. New York: Hill and Wang, 1963.
Adams, Hazard and Leroy Searle, eds. *Critical Theory Since 1965*. Tallahassee: Florida State UP, 1986.
Alegría, Ricardo E. "El grito de 'Fuente Ovejuna lo hizo' en Puerto Rico en 1542, tres cuartos de siglo, antes de Lope de Vega escribir su comedia," *Revista del Centro de Estudios Avanzados de Puerto Rico y el Caribe* 11 (1990): 86-93.
Alston, William P. *Philosophy of Language*. Englewood Cliffs, NJ: Prentice-Hall, 1964.
Andrachuk, Gregory Peter. "'He That Eateth of This Bread Shall Live Forever' (John 6:58): Lázaro's Communion." *Romance Notes* 31 (1991): 205-13.
Archer, Robert. "El pueblo, los reyes y el público: El pragmatismo dramático en *Fuente Ovejuna*." *Voz Hispánica* (1990): 109-19.
Arendt, Hannah. *The Life of the Mind: One / Thinking, Two / Willing*. 2 vols. New York: Harcourt Brace Jovanovich, [*Thinking*] 1971, [*Willing*] 1978.
Anciaux, Paul. *The Sacrament of Penance*. New York: Sheed and Ward, 1962.
Arteaga, Alfred. "An Other Tongue." In Arteaga, ed., *An Other Tongue*. Durham, NC: Duke UP, 1994: 9-33.
Aubrun, Charles Vincent. *La comedia española, 1600-1680*. Madrid: Vaurus, 1968.
Augustine, Saint. *The Confessions of Augustine*. Eds. John Gibb and William Montgomery. New York: Garland Publishing, 1980.
Austin, Gilbert. *Chironomia or A Treatise on Rhetorical Delivery*. Ed. Mary Margaret Robb and Lestor Thonssen. Carbondale and Edwardsville: Southern Illinois UP, 1966 [1806].
Austin, J. L. [Excerpts from] *How to Do Things with Words*. *Critical Theory Since 1965*. Ed. Hazard Adams and Leroy Searle. Tallahassee: Florida State UP, 1986. 833-8.
Axthelm, Peter M. *The Modern Confessional Novel*. New Haven, Connecticut: Yale UP, 1967.
Bakhtin, Mikhail M. [Excerpts from] *Discourse in the Modern Novel*. *Critical Theory Since 1965*. Ed. Hazard Adams and Leroy Searle. Tallahassee: Florida State UP, 1986. 665-78.
Barnett, Dene. *The Art of Gesture*: The Practices and Principles of Eighteenth Century Acting (Heidelberg: Carl Winter, 1987).
Berggren, Erik. *The Psychology of Confessions*. Leiden, the Netherlands: E. J. Brill, 1975.
Bilinkoff, Jodi. "Confessors, Penitents, and the Construction of Identities in Early Modern Avila." *Culture and Identity in Early Modern Europe: 1500-1800*. Ed. Barbara B. Diefendorf and Carla Hesse. Ann Arbor: U of Michigan P, 1993. 83-100.
———. "The Many 'Lives' of Pedro de Ribadeneyra." *Renaissance Quarterly* 52.1 (1999): 180-96.
Blumenberg, Hans. "Light as a Metaphor for Truth: At the Preliminary Stage of Philosophical Concept Formation." *Modernity and the Hegemony of Vision*. Ed. David Michael Levin. Trans. Joel Anderson. Berkeley: U of California P, 1993. 30-62.
Boer, Wietse de. "The Politics of the Soul: Confession in Counter-Reformation Milan." *Penitence*. 116-33.
Borges, Jorge Luis. "Tema del traidor y del héroe." *Ficciones*. Madrid: Alianza Editorial, 2001 [1944]: 146-52.

Bovill, E. W. *The Battle of Alcazar: An Account of the Defeat of Don Sebastian of Portugal of El-Ksar el-Kebir*. London: Batchworth Press, 1952.

Brooks, Peter. *Troubling Confessions: Speaking Guilt in Law and Literature*. Chicago: U of Chicago P, 2000.

Brewer's Dictionary of Phrase and Fable. Ed. Ivor H. Evans. New York: Harper & Rowe, 1981 [1817].

Cañadas, Ivan. "Class, Gender and Community in Thomas Dekker's *The Shoemaker's Holiday* and Lope de Vega's *Fuente Ovejuna*." *Parergon: Journal of the Australian and New Zealand Association for Medieval and Early Modern Studies*. 19.2 (2002): 119-50.

Carey, Douglas M. and Phillip G. Williams. "Religious Confession as Perspective and Mediation in Unamuno's *San Manuel Bueno, mártir*." *Modern Language Notes* 91 (1976): 292-310.Abrams, M.H. *A Glossary of Literary Terms*. 4th ed. New York: Holt, Rinehart and Winston, 1981.

Casa, Frank P., Luciano García Lorenzo, and Germán Vega García-Luengos, eds. *Diccionario de la comedia del Siglo de Oro*. Madrid: Editorial Castalia, 2002.

Castilla, Alberto. "Conflictos sociales." *Diccionario*. 85-87.

Cervantes, Miguel de. *The Adventures of Don Quixote de la Mancha*. Trans. Tobias Smollett. New York: Farrar, Straus and Giroux, 1986 [1605, 1615].

———. *Don Quijote de la Mancha*. Ed. Martín de Riquer. Barcelona: Planeta, 2000 [1605, 1615].

Chacel, Rosa. *La confesión*. Barcelona: Edhasa, 1971.

Cohen, Walter. *Drama of a Nation: Public Theater in Renaissance England and Spain*. Ithaca, New York: Cornell UP, 1985.

"The Council of Trent." Hanover Historical Texts Project. http://history.hanover.edu/texts/texts/trent.html. Accessed 25 July 2007.

Critchley, MacDonald. *Silent Language*. London: Butterworths, 1975.

Cuddon, J. A. *The Penguin Dictionary of Literary Terms and Literary Theory*. 4th ed. New York: Penguin Putnam, 1998.

Davis, Steven. "Perlocutions." In John R. Searle, Ferenc Kiefer and Manfred Bierwisch, eds. *Speech Act Theory and Pragmatics*. 37-55.

Derrida, Jacques. *Acts of Religion*. Ed. Gil Anidjar. New York: Routledge, 2002.

———. *Memoirs of the Blind: The Self-Portrait and Other Ruins*. Trans. Pascale-Anne Brault and Michael Naas. Chicago: U of Chicago P, 1993.

Dixon, Victor. "'Su majestad habla, en fin, como quien tanto ha acertado': La conclusión ejemplar de *Fuente Ovejuna*." *Criticón*. 42 (1988): 155-68.

Doody, Terrence. *Confession and Community in the Novel*. Baton Rouge: Louisiana State UP, 1980.

Dunn, Peter N. "Honor/Honra." *Diccionario*. 166-67.

Escudero Baztán, Juan Manuel. "Villanos." *Diccionario*. 317-18.

Fiore, Robert L. *Drama and Ethos: Natural-Law Ethics in Spanish Golden Age Theater*. Lexington: UP of Kentucky, 1975.

———. "Ley natural." *Diccionario*. 192-93.

Fischer, Susan L. "Fuente Ovejuna on the Rack: Interrogation of a Carnivalesque Theater of Terror." *Hispanic Review* 65.1 (1997): 61-92.

Flynn, Thomas R. "Foucault and the Eclipse of Vision.," *Modernity and the Hegemony of Vision*. Ed. David Michael Levin. Berkeley: U of California P, 1993. 273-86.

Foster, Dennis A. *Confession and Complicity in Narrative*. Cambridge: Cambridge UP, 1987.
Foucault, Michel. *Discipline and Punish: The Birth of the Prison*. 1975. Trans. Alan Sheridan. New York: Random House, 1977 [1975].
———. *The Birth of the Clinic: An Archaeology of Medical Perception*. Trans. A. M. Sheridan Smith. [1973]; New York: Vintage Books, 1994.
"Fourth Lateran Council - 1215 A.D." *Daily Catholic*. http://www.dailycatholic.org/history/12ecume2.htm#On%20yearly%20confession%20to%20one's%20own%20priest,%20yearly%20communion,%20the%20confessional%20seal. Accessed 24 May 2007.
Fox, Dian. "Nobles." *Diccionario*. 226-27.
Friedman, Edward H. "Sangre." *Diccionario*. 267-68.
Fuentes, Carlos. "Introduction." In Miguel de Cervantes, *The Adventures of Don Quixote de la Mancha*, trans. Tobias Smollett. New York: Farrar, Straus and Giroux, 1986. xv-xxxi.
Garcés, María Antonia. *Cervantes in Algiers: A Captive's Tale*. Nashville: Vanderbilt UP, 2002.
Gramsci, Antonio. *Letters from prison* [*Lettere dal carcere*]. Ed. Frank Rosengarten; Trans. Raymond Rosenthal. New York: Columbia UP, 1994.
Greenfield, Summer M. "La 'iglesia' terrestre de *San Manuel Bueno*." *Cuadernos Hispanoamericanos* 348 (1979): 609-20.
Gutiérrez, Luis. *Cornelia Bororquia o la víctima de la Inquisición*. Gérard Dufour, ed. Alicante: Instituto de Estudios, 1987 [1799, 1800].
Hall, J. B. *Lope de Vega: Fuente Ovejuna. Critical Guides to Spanish Texts*. Vol. 42. London: Grant and Culter, 1985.
Hawthorne, Jeremy. *A Glossary of Contemporary Literary Theory*. London: Edward Arnold, 1992.
Hayes, Francis C. *Lope de Vega*. New York: Twayne, 1967.
Hernández Araico, Susana. "Gracioso." *Diccionario*. 160-62.
Hesse, Everett W. *The Comedia and Points of View*. Potomac, Maryland: Scripta Humanistica, 1984.
Icaza, Francisco A. de. *Lope de Vega: Sus amores y sus odios, y otros estudios*. Ed. Ermilo Abreu Gómez. Mexico, D. F.: Editorial Porrúa, 1962 [1925].
Iser, Wolfgang. "The Repertoire." In Hazard Adams and Leroy Searle, eds. *Critical Theory Since 1965*. 360-80.
Jesús, Santa Teresa de. *Libro de la vida*. Ed. Otger Steggink. Madrid: Clásicos Castalia, 1986.
Kirby, Carol Bingham. "Historia." *Diccionario*. 165-66.
Larson, Catherine. "Metatheater and the *Comedia*: Past, Present, and Future. 204-21. The *Golden Age Comedia: Text, Theory, and Performance*. Ed. Charles Ganelin and Howard Mancing. West Lafayette: Purdue UP, 1994.
Lázaro Carreter, Fernanco. *Lope de Vega, introducción a su vida y obra*. Salamanca: Ediciones Anaya, 1966.
Lauer, A. Robert. "Rey." *Diccionario*. 259-61.
Levin, David Michael. "Introduction." *Modernity and the Hegemony of Vision*. Ed. David Michael Levin. Berkeley: U of California P, 1993. 1-29.
———, ed. *Modernity and the Hegemony of Vision*. Berkeley: U of California P, 1993.
Levin, Susan M. *The Romantic Art of Confession: DeQuincey, Musset, Sand, Lamb, Hogg, Frémy, Soulié, Janin*. Columbia, South Carolina: Camden House, 1998.

Low, Anthony. "Privacy, Community, and Society: Confession as a Cultural Indicator in *Sir Gawain and the Green Knight*." *Religion and Literature* 30.2 (1998): 1-20.
Lualdi, Katharine Jackson, and Anne T. Thayer. *Penitence in the Age of Reformations.* Aldershot, U.K.: Ashgate, 2000.
Lualdi, Katharine Jackson, and Anne T. Thayer. "Introduction." *Penitence.* 1-9.
Maher, Michael. "Confession and Consolation: the Society of Jesus and Its Promotion of the General Confession." *Penitence.* 184-200.
Martín Gaite, Carmen. *La búsqueda de interlocutor y otras búsquedas.* Madrid: Nostromo, 1973.
———. *El cuento de nunca acabar.* Madrid: Trieste, 1983.
———. *Retahílas.* Barcelona: Destino, 1974.
McCumber, John. "Derrida and the Closure of Vision." *Modernity and the Hegemony of Vision.* Ed. David Michael Levin. Berkeley: U of California P, 1993. 234-51.
McKendrick, Melveena. *Theater in Spain, 1490-1700.* Cambridge: Cambridge UP, 1989.
Menéndez y Pelayo, Marcelino. *Antología General de Menéndez Pelayo: Recopilación orgánica de su doctrina.* 2 vols. Madrid: Católica, 1956.
Montesinos, José F. *Estudios sobre Lope de Vega.* Salamanca: Ediciones Anaya, 1967.
Motsch, Wolfgang. "Situational Context and Illocutionary Force." In John R. Searle, Ferenc Kiefer and Manfred Bierwisch, eds. *Speech Act Theory and Pragmatics.* 155-68.
Moulin, Bernard, and Daniel Rousseau. "An Approach for Modelling and Simulating Conversations." *Essays in Speech Act Theory.* Ed. Daniel Vanderveken and Susumu Kubo. Philadelphia: John Benjamins, 2002. 175-206.
Nepaulsingh, Colbert I. "In Search of a Tradition, not a Source, for *San Manuel Bueno, mártir*." *Revista Canadiense de Estudios Hispánicos* 11.2 (Winter 1987): 315-30.
Noriega Cantú, Alfonso. *El humorismo en la obra de Lope de Vega.* Mexico, D. F.: Universidad Nacional Autónoma de México, 1976.
Ortiz, Mario A. "*San Manuel bueno, mártir*: Divina novela de Miguel de Unamuno, archimensajero." *Letras Peninsulares* 13.2-3 (Fall 2000-Winter 2001): 725-38.
Pace, D. Gene. "Borges juega con la literatura confessional: 'Tema del traidor y del héroe' y 'Deutsches Requiem.'" *The Latin Americanist* 48.1 (Fall 2004): 23-44.
———. "The Confessant of La Mancha: Don Quixote's Personal and National Pilgrimage." *Framing the Quixote: 1605-2005.* Ed. Alvin F. Sherman, Jr. Provo, Utah: Brigham Young University Department of Spanish and Portuguese, 2007.
———. "¡Es de Lope": The Drama of Confession and *Fuente Ovejuna*." *Bulletin of the Comediantes* 60.1 (2008): 31-50.
———. "Forced Political Confession: Buero Vallejo's *El sueño de la razón*." *Romance Quarterly* 53:2 (Spring 2006): 129-43.
———. "Unfettering Confession: Ritualized Performance in Spanish Narrative and Drama." diss., U of Kentucky, 2005.
Paolini, Shirley Joan. "Towards an Understanding of the Self: The Confessional Mode in Dante's *Commedia* and St. Augustine's *Confessions*." diss., U of California, Irvine, 1973.
Parker, Charles H. "The Rituals of Reconciliation: Admonition, Confession and Community in the Dutch Reformed Church." *Penitence.* 101-15.
Parr, James A. "Tragicomedia." *Diccionario.* 307-09.
Prince, Gerald. "Introduction to the Study of the Narratee." In *Narratology: An Introduction.* Ed. Susana Onega and José Ángel García Landa. London and New York: Longman, 1996.

———. "The Narratee Revisited." *Style* 19.3 (Fall 1985): 299-303.
Quintilian. *Quintilian: The Orator's Education [Institutio Oratoria]*. Ed. and trans. Donald A. Russell. 5 vols. Cambridge: Harvard UP, 2001.
Rades y Andrada, Fray Francisco de. *Crónica de la Orden de Calatrava*. Toledo: Juan de Ayala, 1572.
Rennert, Hugo Albert. *The Life of Lope de Vega (1562-1635)*. New York: Benjamin Blom, 1968.
Rhodes, Elizabeth. "What's in a Name: On Teresa of Ávila's *Book*." *The Mystical Gesture: Essays on Medieval and Early Modern Spiritual Culture*. Ed. Robert Boenig. Burlington, VT: Ashgate, 2000. 79-106.
Ribbans, G. W. "Significado y estructura de 'Fuenteovejuna.'" Trans. Horacio Martínez. *El teatro de Lope de Vega*. Ed. José Francisco Gatti. Buenos Aires: Editorial Universitaria de Buenos Aires, 1962. 91-123. Reprint of "The Meaning and Structure of Lope's *Fuenteovejuna*," *Bulletin of Hispanic Studies* 31 (1954): 150-70.
Ricoeur, Paul. "The Metaphorical Process as Cognition, Imagination, and Feeling." *Critical Theory Since 1965*. Ed. Hazard Adams and Leroy Searle. Tallahassee: Florida State UP, 1986. 424-34.
Root, Jerry. *"Space to Speke": The Confessional Subject in Medieval Literature*. New York: Peter Lang, 1997.
Rose, Constance. "Corte y aldea." *Diccionario*. 91-93.
Rosenberg, John R. *The Circular Pilgrimage and Anatomy of Confessional Autobiography in Spain*. New York: Peter Lang, 1994.
Rousseau, Jean-Jacques. *The Confessions*. Trans. J. M. Cohen. Baltimore: Penguin, 1953 [1781].
Rueda, Ana. "Carmen Martín Gaite: Nudos de interlocución ginergética." En Alfonso de Toro y Dieter Ingenschay, eds., *La novela española actual: autores y tendencias*. Kassel: Edition Reichenberger, 1995.
———. *Cartas sin lacrar: La novela epistolar y la España Ilustrada, 1789-1840*. Madrid: Iberoamericana, 2001.
Ruiz, Juan. *Libro de buen amor*. Ed. Alberto Blecua. 5th ed. Madrid: Cátedra, 2001.
Ruiz Ramón, Francisco. *Historia del teatro español, desde sus orígenes hasta 1900*. Madrid: Cátedra, 2000.
Russell, Donald A., ed. and trans. *Quintilian: The Orator's Education [Institutio Oratoria]*. 5 vols. Cambridge: Harvard UP, 2001.
Searle, John R. *Expression and Meaning: Studies in the Theory of Speech Acts*. Cambridge: Cambridge UP, 1979.
———. "What Is a Speech Act." *Critical Theory Since 1965*. Ed. Hazard Adams and Leroy Searle. Tallahassee: Florida State UP, 1986. 60-9.
Searle, John R., Ferenc Kiefer and Manfred Bierwisch, eds. *Speech Act Theory and Pragmatics*. Dordrecht, Holland: D. Reidel, 1980.
Selwyn, Jennifer D. "'Schools of Mortification': Theatricality and the Role of Penitential Practice in the Jesuits' Popular Missions." *Penitence*. 201-21.
Sender, Ramón J. *Réquiem por un campesino español*. 1950. Barcelona: Ediciones Destino, 1994.
Spires, Robert C. *Post-Totalitarian Spanish Fiction*. Columbia and London: U of Missouri P, 1996.
Spitzer, Leo. "A Central Theme and its Structural Equivalent in Lope's 'Fuenteovejuna.'" *Leo Spitzer: Representative Essays*. Ed. Alban K. Forcione, Herbert Lindenberger, and Madeline Sutherland. Stanford: Stanford UP, 1988. 397-420. Reprint of "A

Central Theme and its Structural Equivalent in Lope's 'Fuenteovejuna.'" *Hispanic Review* 23 (1955): 274-92.

Sullivan, Henry W. "Law, Desire, and the Double Plot: Toward a Psychoanalytic Poetics of the *Comedia*." *The Golden Age Comedia: Text, Theory, and Performance*. Ed. Charles Ganelin and Howard Mancing. West Lafayette: Purdue UP, 1994. 222-35.

Tentler, Thomas N. "Postscript." *Penitence*. 240-59.

———. *Sin and Confession on the Eve of the Reformation*. Princeton: Princeton UP, 1977.

Thayer, Anne T. "Judge and Doctor: Images of the Confessor in Printed Model Sermon Collections, 1450-1520." *Penitence*. 10-29.

Tofanelli, John L. "The Gothic Confessional: Language and Subjectivity in the Gothic Novel, *Villette*, and *Bleak House*." diss., Stanford U, 1987.

Unamuno, Miguel de. *Saint Emmanuel the Good, Martyr*. Trans. and intro. Anthony Kerrigan. 1930; In *Abel Sanchez and Other Stories*. Washington, D.C.: Regnery Gateway, 1956. 207-67.

———. *San Manuel Bueno, mártir*. Ed. Mario J. Valdés. Madrid: Cátedra, 1979 [1930].

Vanderveken, Daniel. "Universal Grammar and Speech Act Theory." Essays in Speech Act Theory. *Ed. Daniel Vanderveken and Susumu Kubo. Philadelphia: John Benjamins, 2002*. 25-62.

Vanderveken, Daniel and Susumu Kubo. "Introduction." Essays in Speech Act Theory. *Ed. Daniel Vanderveken and Susumu Kubo. Philadelphia: John Benjamins, 2002*. 1-22.

———, eds. *Essays in Speech Act Theory*. Amsterdam: John Benjamins, 2002.

Vega Carpio, Félix Lope de. *Arte nuevo de hacer comedias en este tiempo*. http://www.cervantesvirtual.com/servlet/SirveObras/01159174321149352989924/p0000001.htm#I_1. Accessed 29 July 2007.

———. *Four Plays by Lope de Vega*. Ed. and trans. John Garrett Underhill. New York: Charles Scribner's Sons, 1936.

———. *Fuenteovejuna*. Ed. Francisco López Estrada. Madrid: Clásicos Castalia, 1996.

———. *Fuenteovejuna y Peribañez y el Comendador de Ocaña*. Ed. F. García Pavón. 3rd ed. Madrid: Taurus. 1967.

———. *El mejor alcalde, el rey*. Ed. Núria Roig Fisas and Bienvenido Morros. Madrid: Espasa Calpe, 1989.

———. *Peribañez y Fuenteovejuna*. Ed. F. García Pavón. 3rd ed. Madrid: Taurus. 1967.

———. *Peribañez y Fuente Ovejuna*. Ed. Alberto Blecua. Madrid: Alianza, 1981.

———. *The Sheep Well*. *The Golden Age*. Vol. 1. Ed. Norris Houghton. Trans. Angel Flores and Muriel Kittel. New York: Dell, 1963 [1957]: 19-78.

Westminster College (Wilmington, PA). "Theatre Westminster Presents 'Baker from Madrigal." 15 April 2004. http://www.westminster.edu/news/releases/release.fm?id=75.

Wilson, Thomas. *The Arte of Rhetorique*. Ed. G. H. Mair. Oxford: Clarendon P, 1909 [1553].

Young, Richard A. *La figura del rey y la institución real en la comedia lopesca*. Madrid: Ediciones José Porrúa Turanzas, 1979.

Zambrano, María. *La confesión: género literario*. Madrid: Ediciones Siruela, 1995.

Ziomek, Henry K. *A History of Spanish Golden Age Drama*. Lexington, Kentucky: UP of Kentucky, 1984.

Zorrilla, José. *Traidor, inconfeso y mártir*. 1849; Madrid: Teatro Español, 1993.

About the Author

Dr. Donald Gene Pace is professor of History and Spanish at Claflin University, in Orangeburg, South Carolina. He has earned BA (Spanish) and MA (history) degrees from Brigham Young University; a PhD (history) from Ohio State University; and MA (political science), MA (Hispanic literature), and PhD (Hispanic literature) degrees from the University of Kentucky. He has taught at the college level for over a quarter century (history, Spanish, political science), and has been either a division or department chair for much of that time. An associate editor of *Essays in Economic and Business History*, Dr. Pace has published on a wide variety of topics in the areas of Hispanic literature, global health, environmental policy, and history (American West, Latin America, and world). His publications have appeared in many books and journals, including *Bulletin of the Comediantes, Romance Quarterly, Latin Americanist, Hispanic Journal, Essays in Economic and Business History, Brigham Young University Studies, Journal of the West, Journal of Infection in Developing Countries, Indian Journal of Medical Research, and Nature Medicine*. A native of Salt Lake City, Utah, he and his wife, Deone Budge Pace, currently live in Lexington, South Carolina with seven of their fifteen children.